DECODING AI
A Layman's Guide to Understanding Artificial Intelligence

PREFACE

Welcome to "Decoding AI: A Layman's Guide to Understanding Artificial Intelligence." In an age where technology is evolving at an unprecedented pace, artificial intelligence (AI) stands out as one of the most transformative and influential fields of our time. From the way we interact with our devices to the advancements in healthcare and autonomous vehicles, AI is shaping our world in ways we could hardly have imagined a few decades ago.

This book is designed to be a comprehensive yet accessible introduction to the complex and fascinating world of AI. Our goal is to demystify artificial intelligence and make its concepts understandable for everyone, regardless of their technical background. Whether you're a curious reader eager to understand the technology driving your smart assistant or a professional seeking to grasp the fundamentals of AI, this guide is for you.

Why This Book?

Artificial intelligence can seem overwhelming due to its intricate algorithms, jargon, and rapid advancements. With this book, we aim to bridge the gap between the technical complexities of AI and everyday understanding. We believe that everyone should have the opportunity to engage with and benefit from AI knowledge, and our approach is tailored to make these concepts accessible and engaging.

What to Expect

Throughout this book, we will explore:

- **The Basics of AI:** What artificial intelligence is, including its key concepts and historical evolution.

- **The Impact of AI:** How AI affects our daily lives, from smart assistants and recommendation systems to healthcare and autonomous vehicles.

- **Technological Foundations:** An overview of algorithms, models, and the crucial role of data in AI.

- **Ethical and Societal Implications:** The challenges and responsibilities associated with AI, including issues of bias, privacy, and job displacement.

- **The Future of AI:** Emerging trends, the potential for human-AI collaboration, and ethical considerations for responsible development.

We have included practical examples, real-world case studies, and hands-on resources to help you not only understand AI but also see its applications in action. The book is structured to build your knowledge progressively, from foundational principles to more advanced topics, while maintaining clarity and relevance.

Acknowledgements

This book represents the collective effort of many contributors in the field of artificial intelligence, whose research, insights, and innovations have shaped our understanding of this dynamic field. We also extend our gratitude to the readers whose curiosity drives us to share knowledge and inspire learning.

Join Us on This Journey

As you delve into the chapters of "Decoding AI," we encourage you to approach the material with curiosity and an open mind. AI is not just a field for experts but a transformative force that is increasingly integral to our lives. By understanding its principles and applications, you are better equipped to engage with the future and make informed decisions about the technology that will shape our world.

Thank you for choosing to explore AI with us. We hope this book enriches your understanding and ignites a lasting interest in one of the most exciting frontiers of modern science and technology.

Happy reading!

Muhammad Ahmad Zubair Sarwar

Table of Contents

1 INTRODUCTION TO AI

Artificial Intelligence (AI) is a branch of computer science aimed at creating machines that can perform tasks that typically require human intelligence. These tasks include things like understanding natural language, recognizing patterns, solving problems, and making decisions.

In other words, AI is about making computers or software smart enough to think and learn like humans do.

1.1 DEFINITIONS AND BASIC CONCEPTS

1.1.1 MACHINE LEARNING

What it is: Machine Learning is a subset of AI that focuses on teaching computers to learn from data. Instead of being programmed with specific instructions, a machine learning system improves its performance by analyzing patterns in data.

Example: If you have an email system that can filter out spam, it likely uses machine learning to identify and block unwanted emails based on patterns it has learned from previous emails

1.1.2 DEEP LEARNING

What it is: Deep Learning is a specialized area within machine learning that uses neural networks to analyze data. Neural networks are inspired by the human brain and are made up of layers of interconnected nodes (or "neurons") that process information.

Example: Deep learning is used in image recognition systems, like those that can identify objects or people in photos.

1.1.3 NATURAL LANGUAGE PROCESSING (NLP)

What it is: Natural Language Processing is a field of AI that helps computers understand, interpret, and respond to human language in a way that is both meaningful and useful.

Example: Voice assistants like Siri or Alexa use NLP to understand and respond to your spoken commands.

1.1.4 ROBOTICS

What it is: Robotics is the branch of AI that involves designing and building robots. Robots use AI to perform tasks in the real world, such as assembling products or exploring distant planets.

Example: Robotic vacuum cleaners use AI to navigate around obstacles and clean your floor efficiently.

1.1.5   ALGORITHMS

What they are: Algorithms are sets of instructions or rules that a computer follows to solve problems or perform tasks. In AI, algorithms are used to process data and make decisions.

Example: An algorithm might be used to recommend movies based on what you've watched before

1.1.6   WHY AI MATERS

Enhances Efficiency: AI can perform tasks more quickly and accurately than humans in many cases.

Improves Decision Making: AI systems can analyze large amounts of data to help make better decisions.

Creates New Possibilities: AI opens up new opportunities in fields like healthcare, transportation, and entertainment.

In summary, AI is about creating machines that can mimic human intelligence. Through techniques like machine learning, deep learning, and natural language processing, AI systems are able to perform tasks and solve problems in ways   that make our lives easier and more efficient.

1.2   HISTORY AND EVOLUTION OF AI

Artificial Intelligence (AI) has a fascinating history that stretches back over several decades. Understanding its evolution can help us appreciate how far we've come and where we might be heading in the future. Let's break down the journey of AI into easy-to-understand milestones.

1.2.1   EARLY IDEAS AND FOUNDATIONS

1950s: The Birth of AI

Alan Turing: Often considered the father of AI, Turing proposed the idea that machines could think like humans. He introduced the "Turing Test" to determine if a machine's behavior could be indistinguishable from that of a human.

Dartmouth Conference (1956): This event is often credited as the official birth of AI as a field. Researchers like John McCarthy, Marvin Minsky, and others coined the term "artificial intelligence" and laid the groundwork for future AI research.

1.2.2   THE EARLY YEARS: EXCEITEMENTS AND CHALLENGES

1960s-1970s: The First AI Programs

Early Successes: Early AI research produced some notable successes, such as programs that could play chess or solve algebra problems. These programs were rule-based and used specific instructions to achieve their goals.

Limited Progress: Despite early enthusiasm, AI research faced significant challenges. The technology of the time was not advanced enough, and AI systems often struggled with complex problems or lacked the flexibility to handle unexpected situations.

1.2.3 THE WINTER PERIODS

1970s-1980s: AI Winters

Funding Cuts and Reduced Interest: Due to the limitations of early AI systems and unmet expectations, funding for AI research was reduced. This period, known as the "AI Winter," saw a slowdown in progress and interest in the field.

Challenges: Researchers encountered difficulties with scaling their algorithms and dealing with the complexity of real-world problems.

1.2.4 RESURGENCE AND BREAKTHROUGHS

1980s-1990s: Renewed Interest and Innovation

Expert Systems: In the 1980s, AI research saw a revival with the development of expert systems. These systems were designed to mimic the decision-making abilities of human experts in specific domains, like medical diagnosis or financial forecasting.

Machine Learning: The focus began shifting towards machine learning, where computers could improve their performance by learning from data. This was a significant departure from the rule-based systems of the past.

1.2.5 THE MODERN ERA: AI EVERYWHERE

2000s-Present: AI Goes Mainstream

Big Data and Computing Power: The advent of big data and powerful computers provided a boost to AI research. Researchers could now analyze vast amounts of data and train more complex models.

Deep Learning: The development of deep learning, a subset of machine learning that uses neural networks with many layers, led to breakthroughs in image and speech recognition. For instance, AI systems can now identify objects in photos or understand spoken language with high accuracy.

AI in Everyday Life: AI applications have become common in everyday life. From virtual assistants like Siri and Alexa to recommendation systems on streaming platforms, AI is integrated into many aspects of modern life.

1.2.6 CURRENT TRENDS AND FUTURE DIRECTIONS

AI in Various Fields: AI is now making an impact in diverse areas such as healthcare, finance, transportation, and entertainment. Innovations like self-driving cars, personalized medicine, and smart home devices showcase the potential of AI to transform industries.

Ethical and Social Considerations: As AI technology advances, there are increasing discussions about its ethical implications, such as privacy concerns, job displacement, and the need for responsible AI development.

1.2.7 SUMMARY

The journey of AI has been one of highs and lows, with periods of intense excitement and times of challenge. From its early theoretical concepts and initial successes to its current widespread applications and ongoing advancements, AI has evolved significantly. Understanding this history helps us appreciate the progress made and anticipate the future developments in this exciting field.

1.3 IMPACT ON DAILY LIFE AND SOCIETY

Artificial Intelligence (AI) is transforming many aspects of our daily lives and society at large. Its influence is becoming increasingly pervasive, changing how we work, communicate, and interact with the world. Here's a look at how AI is making an impact:

1.3.1 ENHANCING DAILY CONVENIENCE

- Smart Assistants:
  - ✓ Voice-Activated Helpers: AI-powered smart assistants like Siri, Alexa, and Google Assistant make it easier to manage daily tasks. You can set reminders, check the weather, play music, or even control smart home devices just by speaking.
  - ✓ Personalized Experience: These assistants learn from your interactions to provide more personalized responses and recommendations.
- Recommendation Systems:
  - ✓ Entertainment and Shopping: AI algorithms help recommend movies, music, and products based on your preferences. Services like Netflix and Amazon use these systems to suggest content or products that you might like, making your experience more enjoyable and tailored.
- Navigation and Travel:
  - ✓ Real-Time Traffic Updates: AI-driven navigation apps like Google Maps and Waze provide real-time traffic updates and route suggestions, helping you avoid delays and reach your destination more efficiently.
  - ✓ Ride-Sharing: Services like Uber and Lyft use AI to match riders with drivers, optimize routes, and predict arrival times, improving convenience and efficiency in urban transportation.

1.3.2 IMPROVING HEALTH AND WELL-BEING

- Healthcare Diagnostics:
  - ✓ Early Detection: AI systems assist doctors in diagnosing diseases by analyzing medical images, detecting patterns, and identifying early signs of conditions like cancer or heart disease.
  - ✓ Personalized Treatment: AI can help develop personalized treatment plans by analyzing a patient's medical history, genetic information, and current health data.

- Fitness and Wellness:
  - ✓ Wearable Devices: AI-powered wearables like fitness trackers and smartwatches monitor your physical activity, heart rate, and sleep patterns, providing insights into your health and fitness levels.
  - ✓ Mental Health: AI chatbots and apps offer support for mental health, providing resources and activities to help manage stress, anxiety, and other emotional challenges.

1.3.3 REVOLUTIONIZING WORK AND PRODUCTIVITY

- Automation:
  - ✓ Routine Tasks: AI automates repetitive and mundane tasks, such as data entry or scheduling, allowing employees to focus on more complex and creative aspects of their work.
  - ✓ Customer Service: AI chatbots handle customer inquiries and support, providing quick responses and freeing up human agents to handle more intricate issues.
- Enhanced Decision-Making:
  - ✓ Data Analysis: AI tools analyze large volumes of data to uncover trends and insights that inform business decisions, from marketing strategies to financial planning.

1.3.4 TRANSFORMING EDUCATION AND LEARNING

- Personalized Learning:
  - ✓ Adaptive Learning Platforms: AI-driven educational platforms adjust the difficulty and style of content based on individual student performance, offering a tailored learning experience.
  - ✓ Smart Tutoring: AI-powered tutors provide additional help and practice in subjects where students need more support, enhancing their learning outcomes.
- Administrative Efficiency:
  - ✓ Streamlined Operations: AI helps educational institutions manage administrative tasks, such as grading and scheduling, making the educational process more efficient.

1.3.5 ADDRESSING GLOBAL CHALLENGES

- Environmental Monitoring:
  - ✓ Climate Change: AI analyzes environmental data to track climate change, predict natural disasters, and develop strategies for sustainability and conservation.
  - ✓ Energy Efficiency: AI optimizes energy consumption in buildings and industrial processes, reducing waste and promoting more sustainable practices.
- Disaster Response:
  - ✓ Emergency Management: AI helps predict and manage natural disasters, such as hurricanes or earthquakes, by analyzing data and coordinating response efforts.

1.3.6 SUMMARY

AI's impact on daily life and society is profound and multifaceted. It enhances convenience, improves health outcomes, boosts productivity, transforms education, and helps address global challenges. As AI continues to advance, its potential to further enrich and transform our lives will only grow, making it an essential part of our modern world.

1.4 REAL-WORLD APPLICATIONS AND BENEFITS

Artificial Intelligence (AI) has moved beyond science fiction into practical, everyday use. Its applications span a wide range of industries and aspects of daily life, offering numerous benefits. Here's a closer look at how AI is being used in the real world and the advantages it brings.

1.4.1 HEALTHCARE

- Medical Diagnosis:
  - ✓ Early Detection: AI algorithms analyze medical images (like X-rays and MRIs) to identify early signs of diseases such as cancer, allowing for earlier and potentially more successful treatments.
  - ✓ Predictive Analytics: AI can predict patient outcomes and potential health risks by analyzing patterns in medical data, helping doctors make informed decisions.
- Personalized Medicine:
  - ✓ Tailored Treatments: AI analyzes genetic information and health records to customize treatment plans for individual patients, improving the effectiveness of therapies and reducing side effects.

1.4.2 FINANCE

- Fraud Detection:
  - ✓ Security Measures: AI systems monitor transactions in real-time to detect and prevent fraudulent activities, safeguarding financial institutions and their customers.
- Algorithmic Trading:
  - ✓ Market Analysis: AI algorithms analyze market trends and execute trades at high speeds, optimizing investment strategies and improving returns.
- Personal Finance Management:
  - ✓ Budgeting Tools: AI-powered apps help users manage their finances by tracking spending, analyzing financial habits, and offering budgeting advice.

1.4.3 TRANSPORTATION

- Autonomous Vehicles:
  - ✓ Self-Driving Cars: AI technology enables vehicles to navigate roads, detect obstacles, and make driving decisions, aiming to enhance safety and reduce human error.

- ✓ Traffic Management: AI systems optimize traffic flow in cities by analyzing traffic patterns and adjusting signals to reduce congestion and improve travel times.
- Public Transit:
  - ✓ Route Planning: AI helps optimize public transportation routes and schedules based on passenger demand and traffic conditions, improving efficiency and service quality.

1.4.4 RETAIL AND E-COMMERCE

- Customer Recommendations:
  - ✓ Personalized Shopping: AI algorithms analyze browsing and purchase history to recommend products tailored to individual preferences, enhancing the shopping experience.
- Inventory Management:
  - ✓ Demand Forecasting: AI predicts product demand and optimizes inventory levels, helping retailers reduce stockouts and overstock situations.
- Chatbots and Customer Service:
  - ✓ 24/7 Support: AI-powered chatbots provide immediate assistance and handle customer inquiries, improving service availability and response times.

1.4.5 EDUCATION

- Adaptive Learning:
  - ✓ Customized Education: AI-driven educational platforms adapt to individual learning styles and paces, offering personalized lessons and exercises that cater to each student's needs.
- Administrative Efficiency:
  - ✓ Streamlining Tasks: AI automates administrative tasks such as grading and scheduling, allowing educators to focus more on teaching and student interaction.

1.4.6 ENTERTAINMENT

- Content Creation:
  - ✓ Creative Tools: AI assists in creating music, art, and literature by generating content based on patterns and styles, providing new tools for creative expression.
- Personalized Media:
  - ✓ Recommendation Engines: AI curates personalized content recommendations for streaming services, helping users discover new movies, shows, and music tailored to their tastes.

1.4.7 ENVIRONMENTAL PROTECTION

- Climate Modeling:
  - ✓ Predictive Analysis: AI models analyze climate data to predict weather patterns and assess the impact of environmental changes, aiding in climate change mitigation and adaptation strategies.
- Resource Management:

✓ Efficiency Improvements: AI optimizes the use of natural resources in agriculture, water management, and energy consumption, promoting sustainability and reducing waste.

1.4.8   MANUFACTURING

- Automation and Robotics:
  ✓ Enhanced Production: AI-powered robots and automation systems improve manufacturing efficiency, precision, and safety, leading to higher-quality products and reduced production costs.
- Predictive Maintenance:
  ✓ Equipment Monitoring: AI analyzes data from machinery to predict potential failures and schedule maintenance before issues arise, minimizing downtime and repair costs.

1.4.9   SUMMARY

AI's real-world applications span numerous industries, offering substantial benefits such as enhanced efficiency, personalized experiences, improved safety, and innovative solutions to complex problems. As AI continues to evolve, its impact will likely expand further, bringing even more advantages to individuals and organizations alike.

2 THE BASICS OF AI

2.1 UNDERSTANDING MACHINE LEARNING

Artificial Intelligence (AI), Machine Learning (ML), and Deep Learning (DL) are related fields but each represents a different level of complexity and capability. Understanding their differences can help clarify how they fit into the broader landscape of technology and data science. Let's break down each concept:

2.1.1 ARTIFICIAL INTELLIGENCE (AI)

- Definition:
  - ✓ Broad Concept: AI is the overarching field that aims to create machines or software that can perform tasks that typically require human intelligence. This includes problem-solving, reasoning, learning, and understanding language.
  - ✓ Goal: The main goal of AI is to develop systems that can mimic or replicate human cognitive functions.
- Scope:
  - ✓ Wide Range: AI encompasses various techniques and methods, including rule-based systems, expert systems, and more advanced approaches like machine learning and deep learning.
- Examples:
  - ✓ Virtual Assistants: Siri and Alexa use AI to understand and respond to user commands.
  - ✓ Game Playing: AI systems like IBM's Deep Blue that play chess at a grandmaster level.

2.1.2 MACHINE LEARNING (ML)

- Definition:
  - ✓ Subset of AI: Machine Learning is a subset of AI focused on developing algorithms that enable computers to learn from and make predictions or decisions based on data.
  - ✓ Learning from Data: Unlike traditional AI, which might rely on predefined rules, ML systems improve their performance by identifying patterns and insights in data.
- Scope:
  - ✓ Data-Driven: ML algorithms learn from historical data and use this knowledge to make predictions or decisions without being explicitly programmed to perform those tasks.
  - ✓ Techniques: Includes supervised learning (e.g., classification and regression), unsupervised learning (e.g., clustering and association), and reinforcement learning.
- Examples:
  - ✓ Email Filtering: ML algorithms classify emails as spam or not spam based on past data.
  - ✓ Recommendation Systems: Platforms like Netflix and Amazon use ML to suggest movies or products based on user preferences and behavior.

2.1.3   DEEP LEARNING (DL)

- Definition:
  - ✓ Subset of ML: Deep Learning is a specialized subset of Machine Learning that involves neural networks with many layers (hence "deep"). These networks are designed to automatically learn and extract features from raw data.
  - ✓ Hierarchical Learning: DL models automatically discover hierarchical patterns in data, allowing them to perform complex tasks with high accuracy.
- Scope:
  - ✓ Complex Data Processing: DL excels at processing large amounts of unstructured data like images, audio, and text. It's particularly powerful in scenarios where traditional ML might struggle.
  - ✓ Neural Networks: Uses deep neural networks (DNNs), including convolutional neural networks (CNNs) for image tasks and recurrent neural networks (RNNs) for sequential data.
- Examples:
  - ✓ Image Recognition: DL models, like those used in Google Photos, can identify and categorize objects or people in images.
  - ✓ Natural Language Processing: DL is used in language models like GPT-3 to generate human-like text and understand complex language patterns.

2.1.4   SUMMARY

- Artificial Intelligence (AI) is the broadest concept, aiming to create systems that perform tasks requiring human-like intelligence.
- Machine Learning (ML) is a subset of AI that focuses on algorithms that learn from data to make predictions or decisions.
- Deep Learning (DL) is a subset of ML that uses multi-layered neural networks to automatically learn and represent complex patterns in data.

Understanding these distinctions helps clarify the capabilities and applications of each technology and their role in advancing artificial intelligence.

2.2   HOW MACHINES LEARN FROM DATA

Machines learn from data through a process that involves analyzing patterns, making predictions, and improving over time based on experience. This process is fundamental to both Machine Learning (ML) and Deep Learning (DL). Here's a straightforward explanation of how this learning process works:

2.2.1   DATA COLLECTION

- Gathering Information:
  - ✓ Data Sources: The first step is collecting relevant data. This can include text, images, numbers, or other forms of information depending on the task.
  - ✓ Quality and Quantity: The quality and quantity of data are crucial. More and better-quality data usually lead to better learning outcomes.

- Examples:
  - ✓ Images: Collecting thousands of labeled images of cats and dogs for a classification task.
  - ✓ Text: Gathering large datasets of text to train a language model.

2.2.2 DATA PREPARATION

- Cleaning and Preprocessing:
  - ✓ Cleaning: Raw data often needs to be cleaned to remove errors, inconsistencies, or irrelevant information.
  - ✓ Preprocessing: Data is then transformed into a format suitable for analysis. This can include normalizing values, encoding categorical variables, or splitting data into training and testing sets.
- Examples:
  - ✓ Images: Resizing or cropping images to a consistent size.
  - ✓ Text: Removing punctuation and converting text to lowercase.

2.2.3 CHOOSING A MODEL

- Selecting an Algorithm:
  - ✓ Model Selection: Depending on the task (e.g., classification, regression, clustering), different algorithms or models are chosen. This could be a simple linear regression model or a complex deep neural network.
  - ✓ Training: The chosen model is then trained on the prepared data.
- Examples:
  - ✓ Classification: Using logistic regression or a neural network for predicting categories.
  - ✓ Regression: Applying linear regression to predict numerical values.

2.2.4 TRAINING THE MODEL

- Learning from Data:
  - ✓ Training Process: During training, the model learns by adjusting its parameters to minimize the difference between its predictions and the actual outcomes. This is done through iterative processes where the model updates its parameters based on the errors it makes.
  - ✓ Optimization Algorithms: Techniques like gradient descent are used to find the best parameters that reduce prediction errors.
- Examples:
  - ✓ Image Classification: A neural network adjusts its weights based on the errors it makes in classifying images as cats or dogs.
  - ✓ Language Processing: A model fine-tunes its ability to predict the next word in a sentence based on vast amounts of text data.

2.2.5 EVALUATING AND TESTING

- Assessing Performance:
  - ✓ Validation: After training, the model's performance is evaluated using a separate set of data that it hasn't seen before (validation or test data). This helps determine how well the model generalizes to new, unseen data.

- ✓ Metrics: Common metrics for evaluation include accuracy, precision, recall, F1 score, and mean squared error, depending on the task.
- Examples:
  - ✓ Classification Accuracy: Measuring how often the model correctly classifies images.
  - ✓ Regression Error: Evaluating how close the model's predictions are to the actual values.

2.2.6 INTERATION AND IMPROVEMENT

- Refinement:
  - ✓ Hyperparameter Tuning: Adjusting parameters that control the learning process, such as learning rate or number of layers, to improve model performance.
  - ✓ Re-training: The model might be retrained with more data or different features to enhance its accuracy and robustness.
- Examples:
  - ✓ Improving Image Recognition: Adding more training data or refining the network architecture to better recognize objects in images.
  - ✓ Enhancing Text Generation: Fine-tuning a language model with more diverse text to improve its fluency and relevance.

2.2.7 SUMMARY

Machines learn from data through a systematic process of collecting and preparing data, choosing and training a model, evaluating its performance, and iteratively improving it. By analyzing patterns and adjusting based on feedback, machine learning systems can make predictions, recognize patterns, and perform tasks that mimic human intelligence.

2.3 TYPES OF AI

Artificial Intelligence (AI) can be categorized into different types based on its scope and capabilities. The two primary types are Narrow AI and General AI. Understanding these distinctions helps clarify the current state of AI technology and its potential future developments.

2.3.1 NARROW AI (WEAK AI)

- Definition:
  - ✓ Specialized Functionality: Narrow AI, also known as Weak AI, is designed to perform a specific task or a set of related tasks. It is focused on a single domain and cannot perform outside its predefined functions.
  - ✓ Task-Specific: Narrow AI systems excel at tasks they are explicitly programmed for but lack the flexibility to handle tasks outside their specialized scope.
- Characteristics:
  - ✓ Limited Scope: Operates within a narrowly defined context or problem area.
  - ✓ Predefined Capabilities: Executes tasks based on predefined rules, patterns, or algorithms.

- ✓ No True Understanding: While it can simulate intelligent behavior, it doesn't possess genuine understanding or consciousness.
- Examples:
  - ✓ Virtual Assistants: Siri, Alexa, and Google Assistant perform specific functions like setting reminders, answering questions, or playing music but cannot handle tasks beyond their programmed capabilities.
  - ✓ Recommendation Systems: Platforms like Netflix and Amazon use Narrow AI to suggest movies or products based on user preferences and previous interactions.
  - ✓ Spam Filters: Email systems use Narrow AI to classify incoming emails as spam or not spam based on patterns in the data.
- Benefits:
  - ✓ Efficiency: Streamlines and automates repetitive tasks, improving productivity.
  - ✓ Accuracy: Often highly accurate within its domain, thanks to targeted algorithms and training.

2.3.2 GENERAL AI (STRONG AI)

- Definition:
  - ✓ Human-Like Intelligence: General AI, also known as Strong AI or Artificial General Intelligence (AGI), refers to a type of AI that possesses the ability to understand, learn, and apply intelligence across a wide range of tasks, similar to human cognitive abilities.
  - ✓ Broad Scope: Unlike Narrow AI, General AI can perform any intellectual task that a human can, making it highly versatile and adaptable.
- Characteristics:
  - ✓ Flexible Learning: Capable of transferring knowledge and skills across different domains.
  - ✓ Autonomous Reasoning: Exhibits the ability to reason, plan, and solve complex problems in various contexts.
  - ✓ Human-Like Understanding: Possesses a level of understanding and cognitive functioning comparable to human intelligence.
- Examples:
  - ✓ Theoretical Concept: As of now, General AI remains a theoretical concept and has not yet been realized in practice. It represents the future goal of AI research and development.
  - ✓ Speculative Scenarios: Science fiction often explores scenarios involving General AI, such as robots with human-like thought processes and emotional understanding.
- Benefits:
  - ✓ Versatility: Can adapt to and perform a wide range of tasks, making it highly flexible and capable of handling complex and dynamic environments.
  - ✓ Enhanced Problem-Solving: Possesses the potential to tackle diverse and unprecedented challenges with creative and autonomous solutions.

2.3.3   SUMMARY

- Narrow AI (Weak AI) refers to systems designed for specific tasks, demonstrating expertise within a narrow domain but lacking general cognitive abilities. It's the type of AI most commonly used today in applications like virtual assistants, recommendation engines, and automated customer service.
- General AI (Strong AI) aims to replicate human-like intelligence and cognitive abilities, allowing for versatile problem-solving and learning across various domains. While it remains a theoretical concept with significant research and development still needed, it represents the ultimate aspiration for AI technology.

Understanding these types of AI helps set realistic expectations about current capabilities and future possibilities, highlighting both the advancements and the challenges in the field of artificial intelligence.

2.4   EXAMPLES OF NARROW AI

Narrow AI, or Weak AI, is designed to perform specific tasks and operates within a limited scope. It excels in its designated function but cannot perform tasks beyond its programmed capabilities. Here are some prominent examples of Narrow AI:

2.4.1   VOICE ASSISTANTS

- Description:
  - ✓ Functionality: Voice assistants are AI systems that use natural language processing (NLP) to understand and respond to spoken commands. They help users perform a range of tasks through voice interaction.
  - ✓ Capabilities: They can answer questions, set reminders, control smart home devices, and more.
- Examples:
  - ✓ Siri: Apple's virtual assistant integrated into iOS devices. Siri can perform tasks like sending texts, setting alarms, and providing weather updates based on voice commands.
  - ✓ Alexa: Amazon's voice assistant used in Echo devices. Alexa can play music, control smart home devices, provide news updates, and even order products online.
  - ✓ Google Assistant: Google's voice assistant available on Android devices and Google Home speakers. It can handle tasks such as navigating, setting reminders, and answering queries.

2.4.2   RECOMMENDATION SYSTEMS

- Description:
  - ✓ Functionality: Recommendation systems use AI algorithms to analyze user behavior and preferences to suggest products, content, or services tailored to individual tastes.
  - ✓ Capabilities: They help enhance user experience by personalizing suggestions based on past interactions and preferences.
- Examples:

- ✓ Netflix: Netflix's recommendation engine suggests movies and TV shows based on a user's viewing history, ratings, and preferences. The system uses collaborative filtering and content-based methods to tailor recommendations.
- ✓ Amazon: Amazon's recommendation system suggests products based on a user's browsing history, previous purchases, and items frequently bought together. It uses machine learning algorithms to personalize shopping experiences.
- ✓ Spotify: Spotify's recommendation engine provides music suggestions based on listening history, favorite genres, and user-created playlists. It uses algorithms like collaborative filtering to recommend new tracks and artists.

2.4.3   SPAM FILTER'S

- Description:
  - ✓ Functionality: Spam filters use AI to identify and block unwanted or potentially harmful emails. They analyze the content of emails and detect patterns associated with spam or phishing attempts.
  - ✓ Capabilities: They help manage email inboxes by filtering out irrelevant or malicious messages, improving email security and user productivity.
- Examples:
  - ✓ Gmail Spam Filter: Gmail's spam filter uses machine learning to classify emails as spam or important based on content, sender reputation, and user interactions. It helps keep users' inboxes clean by moving unwanted emails to the Spam folder.
  - ✓ Outlook Junk Email Filter: Microsoft Outlook's junk email filter employs AI to detect and filter out spam emails, reducing the likelihood of phishing and unwanted advertisements.

2.4.4   CHATBOTS

- Description:
  - ✓ Functionality: Chatbots are AI systems designed to simulate conversation with users, typically through text or voice. They provide automated responses to common queries and perform specific tasks.
  - ✓ Capabilities: They can handle customer service inquiries, provide information, and assist with various tasks through natural language interactions.
- Examples:
  - ✓ Customer Service Chatbots: Many companies use AI chatbots to provide immediate support for common customer queries. For example, banks and retail companies deploy chatbots to assist with account inquiries, order tracking, and service requests.
  - ✓ Healthcare Chatbots: Health-related chatbots, such as those developed by companies like Babylon Health, offer medical advice, symptom checking, and appointment scheduling based on user input.

2.4.5   IMAGE RECOGNITION SYSTEMS

- Description:

- ✓ Functionality: Image recognition systems use AI to analyze and classify visual content. They identify objects, faces, and scenes within images by learning from labeled datasets.
- ✓ Capabilities: They can enhance security, improve user experiences, and automate processes involving visual data.
- Examples:
  - ✓ Facial Recognition: Systems like those used in smartphones for unlocking devices or security cameras for surveillance. They analyze facial features to verify identity.
  - ✓ Google Photos: Google Photos uses image recognition to categorize and search for photos based on their content, such as identifying people, places, and objects in images.

2.4.6   SUMMARY

Narrow AI systems are designed to excel at specific tasks within a defined scope. They are widely used in applications like voice assistants, recommendation systems, spam filters, chatbots, and image recognition. While these systems are highly effective within their domains, they lack the general intelligence and adaptability found in broader AI concepts.

3 KEY TECHNOLOGIES BEHIND AI

3.1 ALGORITHMS

Algorithms are at the heart of Artificial Intelligence (AI). They provide the step-by-step procedures or rules that AI systems use to process data, make decisions, and solve problems. Understanding algorithms is essential for grasping how AI systems operate and improve. Here's an easy-to-understand introduction to algorithms and their workings:

3.1.1 WHAT IS AN ALGORITHM?

- Definition:
  - ✓ Step-by-Step Procedure: An algorithm is a set of instructions or rules designed to perform a specific task or solve a problem. In computing, algorithms are implemented in programming languages to process data and generate outputs.
  - ✓ Deterministic: Algorithms are usually deterministic, meaning they will produce the same output given the same input, following the predefined set of steps.
- Characteristics:
  - ✓ Clear and Unambiguous: Each step in an algorithm should be well-defined and straightforward.
  - ✓ Finite Steps: Algorithms must have a clear end point and not run indefinitely.
  - ✓ Input and Output: Algorithms take input data, process it through defined steps, and produce output.

3.1.2 HOW ALGORITHMS WORK?

- Problem Definition:
  - ✓ Identify the Goal: Determine what problem needs to be solved or what task needs to be performed. This helps define the purpose and requirements of the algorithm.
- Data Input:
  - ✓ Collect and Prepare Data: Input data is collected and formatted according to the needs of the algorithm. This can include raw data, user inputs, or data from sensors.
- Processing:
  - ✓ Execution of Steps: The algorithm processes the input data through a series of predefined steps or calculations. This can involve mathematical operations, data transformations, or logical decisions.
  - ✓ Iterative Process: Many algorithms use iterative methods, where they repeatedly perform a set of operations until a desired outcome is achieved or a condition is met.
- Decision Making:
  - ✓ Conditions and Branching: Algorithms often include conditional statements (like "if-else" conditions) that allow them to make decisions based on the data. This helps tailor the algorithm's behavior to different scenarios.
- Output Generation:

✓ Result Production: After processing the input data, the algorithm generates an output. This could be a solution to a problem, a classification, a recommendation, or any other result based on the algorithm's purpose.
- Evaluation and Adjustment:
  ✓ Performance Assessment: The effectiveness of the algorithm is evaluated based on its output and performance. Metrics such as accuracy, speed, and efficiency are used to assess how well the algorithm meets its goals.
  ✓ Fine-Tuning: Based on evaluation results, the algorithm may be adjusted or optimized to improve performance or adapt to new data or requirements.

3.1.3 TYPES OF ALGORITHMS IN AI?

- Search Algorithms:
  ✓ Purpose: Used to find solutions or paths in search spaces, such as navigating routes or solving puzzles.
  ✓ Example: A* (A-Star) algorithm for finding the shortest path in navigation systems.
- Sorting Algorithms:
  ✓ Purpose: Organize data in a specific order, such as numerical or alphabetical order.
  ✓ Example: Quick Sort and Merge Sort for sorting large datasets efficiently.
- Classification Algorithms:
  ✓ Purpose: Categorize data into predefined classes or labels.
  ✓ Example: Decision Trees and Support Vector Machines (SVMs) used in spam detection or image recognition.
- Regression Algorithms:
  ✓ Purpose: Predict numerical values based on input data.
  ✓ Example: Linear Regression and Polynomial Regression for forecasting trends or making predictions.
- Clustering Algorithms:
  ✓ Purpose: Group similar data points into clusters or groups based on their features.
  ✓ Example: K-Means Clustering and DBSCAN used in customer segmentation or pattern recognition.
- Optimization Algorithms:
  ✓ Purpose: Find the best solution from a set of possible solutions, often under constraints.
  ✓ Example: Gradient Descent used to minimize error in machine learning models.

3.1.4 SUMMARY

Algorithms are fundamental to AI, guiding how data is processed and decisions are made. They consist of a sequence of steps that transform input data into meaningful output. By defining the problem, processing data, making decisions, and evaluating results, algorithms drive the functionality of AI systems. Different types of algorithms cater to various tasks, from sorting and searching to classification and optimization, each playing a crucial role in the broader AI landscape.

3.2 OVERVIEW OF POPULAR AI MODELS

In the field of Artificial Intelligence (AI), various models are employed to solve different types of problems. Each model has its own strengths and is suited for specific tasks. Here's an overview of some popular AI models, including neural networks and decision trees:

3.2.1 NEURAL NETWORKS

- Definition:
  - ✓ Inspiration from Biology: Neural networks are computational models inspired by the human brain's structure and functioning. They consist of interconnected nodes or neurons organized in layers.
  - ✓ Function: These networks learn to perform tasks by processing data through layers of neurons, adjusting connections based on the error of predictions.
- Structure:
  - ✓ Input Layer: Receives the raw input data.
  - ✓ Hidden Layers: Intermediate layers that transform the input data through various functions and learn complex patterns. The depth (number of hidden layers) can vary, leading to different types of neural networks.
  - ✓ Output Layer: Produces the final prediction or classification.
- Types:
  - ✓ Feedforward Neural Networks (FNNs): The simplest type, where data moves in one direction from input to output without looping back.
  - ✓ Convolutional Neural Networks (CNNs): Specialized for image and video processing, CNNs use convolutional layers to detect spatial hierarchies and patterns.
  - ✓ Recurrent Neural Networks (RNNs): Designed for sequential data, such as time series or natural language, RNNs use loops to maintain context and memory across sequences.
- Examples:
  - ✓ Image Classification: CNNs are widely used in applications like facial recognition and object detection.
  - ✓ Language Translation: RNNs and their advanced variants, such as Long Short-Term Memory (LSTM) networks, are used in machine translation systems.

3.2.2 DECISION TREES

- Definition:
  - ✓ Tree-like Model: Decision trees are a type of model that uses a tree structure to make decisions based on feature values. Each node in the tree represents a decision rule, and each branch represents the outcome of that rule.
  - ✓ Function: They make decisions by recursively splitting the data into subsets based on the values of features, leading to different branches of the tree until a final decision is reached.
- Structure:
  - ✓ Root Node: The top node that represents the entire dataset and makes the first split based on a feature.

✓ Decision Nodes: Nodes that represent decisions based on the value of a feature and lead to further splits.
✓ Leaf Nodes: Terminal nodes that provide the final classification or regression result.
- Advantages:
  ✓ Interpretability: Easy to understand and visualize, making it straightforward to see how decisions are made.
  ✓ No Need for Data Scaling: Decision trees do not require normalization or scaling of data.
- Examples:
  ✓ Customer Segmentation: Decision trees can classify customers into different segments based on attributes like age, income, and spending habits.
  ✓ Medical Diagnosis: Used to classify patients based on symptoms and test results.

3.2.3 SUPPORT VECTOR MACHINES (SVMs)

- Definition:
  ✓ Classification Model: SVMs are supervised learning models used for classification and regression tasks. They find the optimal hyperplane that best separates data points of different classes.
  ✓ Function: SVMs maximize the margin between data points of different classes, ensuring that the separation is as wide as possible.
- Types:
  ✓ Linear SVM: Used for linearly separable data.
  ✓ Kernel SVM: Uses kernel functions to handle non-linearly separable data by transforming it into a higher-dimensional space.
- Examples:
  ✓ Text Classification: SVMs are used in spam detection and sentiment analysis.
  ✓ Image Classification: Effective in recognizing patterns and objects in images.

3.2.4 K-Nearest Neighbors (KNN)

- Definition:
  ✓ Instance-Based Learning: KNN is a simple, instance-based learning algorithm used for classification and regression. It classifies a data point based on the majority class of its k-nearest neighbors.
  ✓ Function: Given a new data point, KNN identifies the 'k' closest points from the training dataset and makes predictions based on their labels.
- Advantages:
  ✓ Simplicity: Easy to implement and understand.
  ✓ No Training Phase: KNN does not require a training phase, as it makes decisions based on the entire dataset at prediction time.
- Examples:
  ✓ Recommendation Systems: KNN can be used to recommend products based on the similarity of user preferences.
  ✓ Pattern Recognition: Used in various pattern recognition tasks, such as handwriting recognition.

3.2.5 RANDOM FORESTS

- Definition:
  - ✓ Ensemble Model: Random Forests are an ensemble learning method that combines multiple decision trees to improve prediction accuracy and control overfitting.
  - ✓ Function: It aggregates the results of multiple decision trees, each trained on different subsets of the data and features, to produce a more robust and accurate prediction.
- Advantages:
  - ✓ Robustness: Reduces overfitting and improves generalization by averaging the results of multiple trees.
  - ✓ Feature Importance: Can provide insights into the importance of different features in making predictions.
- Examples:
  - ✓ Credit Scoring: Used to predict the likelihood of a borrower defaulting on a loan.
  - ✓ Medical Diagnosis: Applied to classify medical conditions based on patient data.

3.2.6 SUMMARY

Popular AI models such as neural networks, decision trees, SVMs, KNN, and random forests each have unique characteristics and applications. Neural networks, with their complex structures, excel in tasks involving image and language processing. Decision trees are valued for their interpretability and ease of use in classification and regression. SVMs are effective for classification with clear margins, while KNN provides a simple approach to classification and regression based on proximity. Random Forests enhance decision tree performance by combining multiple trees for improved accuracy. Understanding these models helps in choosing the right approach for specific AI tasks and applications.

3.3 IMPORTANCE OF DATA IN AI

Data is the lifeblood of Artificial Intelligence (AI). It serves as the foundation upon which AI systems are built, trained, and refined. The quality, quantity, and relevance of data significantly influence the performance and effectiveness of AI models. Here's why data is so crucial in AI:

3.3.1 TRAINING AI MODELS

- Learning from Data:
  - ✓ Basis for Learning: AI models, especially those using machine learning (ML) and deep learning, rely on data to learn and make predictions. The model's ability to recognize patterns, make decisions, and generate outputs is directly tied to the data it is trained on.
  - ✓ Example: A neural network trained on images of cats and dogs learns to distinguish between the two by analyzing features such as shape, color, and texture from the provided images.
- Training Process:

✓ Supervised Learning: In supervised learning, labeled data is used to teach the model to map inputs to desired outputs. The more diverse and comprehensive the data, the better the model's ability to generalize and perform well on new, unseen data.

✓ Unsupervised Learning: In unsupervised learning, data is used to find hidden patterns or groupings without predefined labels. The model identifies structures and relationships within the data itself.

3.3.2   ENHANCING MODEL ACCURACY

- Quality Over Quantity:
  - ✓ High-Quality Data: Accurate, clean, and well-labeled data lead to better model performance. Poor quality data can introduce biases, errors, and inaccuracies, affecting the model's ability to make reliable predictions.
  - ✓ Example: A recommendation system using inaccurate user preferences or incomplete product information may make irrelevant suggestions.
- Large Datasets:
  - ✓ Improved Performance: Larger datasets allow models to learn more detailed patterns and variations, improving their accuracy and robustness. More data helps the model understand diverse scenarios and edge cases.
  - ✓ Example: Language models like GPT-3 are trained on vast amounts of text data to generate coherent and contextually relevant text.

3.3.3   PREVENTING OVERFITTING

- Generalization:
  - ✓ Balancing Complexity: A model trained on too little data might learn to perform well on the training data but fail to generalize to new data, a problem known as overfitting. More data helps the model to generalize better, improving its performance on unseen examples.
  - ✓ Example: A spam filter trained on a small dataset might misclassify new types of spam emails, while a filter trained on a large and diverse dataset is more likely to recognize and block them effectively.
- Cross-Validation:
  - ✓ Validation Techniques: Techniques such as cross-validation use multiple subsets of data to test the model's performance, ensuring it generalizes well across different data segments.

3.3.4   ENABLING CONTINUOUS IMPROVEMENT

- Model Updating:
  - ✓ Adapting to Changes: AI models can be continuously improved and updated with new data. This allows them to adapt to changes in patterns, behaviors, and trends over time.
  - ✓ Example: Financial fraud detection systems are updated with new transaction data to recognize emerging fraud patterns and improve their detection capabilities.
- Feedback Loops:

✓ Learning from Errors: Data collected from model predictions and user interactions can be used to fine-tune and enhance the model. Feedback loops help in correcting errors and improving overall performance.

3.3.5 SUPPORTING DIVERSE APPLICATIONS

- Wide Range of Uses:
  - ✓ Versatility: Data supports a wide range of AI applications, from image and speech recognition to predictive analytics and recommendation systems. Each application requires specific types of data to function effectively.
  - ✓ Example: In autonomous vehicles, data from cameras, sensors, and GPS systems is crucial for navigation, object detection, and decision-making.
- Domain-Specific Data:
  - ✓ Custom Solutions: Different industries and applications require domain-specific data. For instance, medical AI systems need patient health records and diagnostic data, while financial AI systems use market data and transaction histories.

3.3.6 SUMMARY

Data is fundamental to the success of AI systems. It drives the training process, enhances model accuracy, prevents overfitting, enables continuous improvement, and supports a diverse range of applications. High-quality, relevant, and ample data ensures that AI models can learn effectively, make accurate predictions, and adapt to evolving scenarios. As AI technology continues to advance, the importance of data in shaping and optimizing AI systems remains central to their development and application.

3.4 DATA COLLECTION, PREPROCESSING, AND USAGE IN AI

In the realm of Artificial Intelligence (AI), the journey from raw data to actionable insights involves several critical steps: data collection, preprocessing, and usage. Each step is crucial for ensuring that AI models are effective, accurate, and reliable. Here's an overview of these steps and their importance:

3.4.1 DATA COLLECTION

- Definition:
  - ✓ Gathering Raw Data: Data collection involves gathering data from various sources to build and train AI models. This step is essential as it provides the foundational input for the entire AI process.
  - ✓ Sources: Data can be collected from numerous sources including databases, sensors, user interactions, web scraping, and external APIs.
- Methods:
  - ✓ Manual Collection: Gathering data through surveys, interviews, or observation. This method is often used when specific and controlled data is required.
  - ✓ Automated Collection: Using tools and scripts to automatically collect data from websites, social media, and other digital platforms.

- ✓ Sensor Data: Collecting data from IoT devices, cameras, or other sensors for real-time monitoring and analysis.
- Considerations:
  - ✓ Relevance: Ensure that the collected data is relevant to the problem being addressed.
  - ✓ Volume: Collect enough data to provide a comprehensive basis for training and evaluation. More data can improve model performance but requires more storage and processing power.
  - ✓ Privacy and Ethics: Respect privacy laws and ethical guidelines, especially when handling personal or sensitive information.

3.4.2 DATA PREPROCESSING

- Definition:
  - ✓ Transforming Raw Data: Data preprocessing involves cleaning, organizing, and transforming raw data into a format suitable for analysis and modeling. This step helps improve the quality and usability of the data.
- Steps:
  - ✓ Data Cleaning:
    - o Handling Missing Values: Address missing or incomplete data by imputing values, using algorithms to estimate missing data, or removing incomplete records.
    - o Removing Duplicates: Eliminate duplicate records to avoid redundancy and ensure data integrity.
    - o Correcting Errors: Fix inaccuracies or inconsistencies in the data, such as typos or incorrect entries.
  - ✓ Data Transformation:
    - o Normalization/Scaling: Adjust numerical data to a standard range or scale to ensure that features contribute equally to the model. For example, scaling data to a range of 0 to 1.
    - o Encoding Categorical Variables: Convert categorical data into numerical format using techniques like one-hot encoding or label encoding, so it can be processed by machine learning algorithms.
    - o Feature Extraction: Create new features from existing data to improve model performance. For instance, extracting keywords from text or deriving new metrics from raw data.
  - ✓ Data Splitting:
    - o Training, Validation, and Test Sets: Split the data into training, validation, and test sets to evaluate the model's performance and ensure it generalizes well to new data. The training set is used to train the model, the validation set to tune parameters, and the test set to assess final performance.

3.4.3 DATA USAGE

- Definition:
  - ✓ Applying Data to AI Models: Once the data is preprocessed, it is used to train, validate, and test AI models. The goal is to leverage the data to create models that can make accurate predictions or classifications.
- Training Models:

- ✓ Algorithm Selection: Choose appropriate algorithms and models based on the nature of the problem and the type of data. For example, use neural networks for image recognition or decision trees for classification tasks.
- ✓ Training Process: Feed the preprocessed data into the model to learn patterns and relationships. Adjust model parameters to optimize performance based on the training data.
- Evaluation and Testing:
  - ✓ Performance Metrics: Assess model performance using metrics like accuracy, precision, recall, F1 score, or mean squared error, depending on the task.
  - ✓ Cross-Validation: Use techniques like k-fold cross-validation to ensure the model performs consistently across different subsets of the data and to avoid overfitting.
- Deployment and Monitoring:
  - ✓ Model Deployment: Integrate the trained model into a production environment where it can make predictions or provide insights based on new data.
  - ✓ Ongoing Monitoring: Continuously monitor the model's performance in real-world scenarios and update it with new data to maintain its accuracy and relevance.

3.4.4 SUMMARY

Data collection, preprocessing, and usage are fundamental steps in the AI pipeline. Data collection involves gathering relevant and sufficient data from various sources. Preprocessing transforms raw data into a clean and usable format, addressing issues like missing values, normalization, and encoding. Finally, data usage encompasses training AI models with preprocessed data, evaluating their performance, and deploying them for practical applications. Proper handling of these steps ensures that AI models are accurate, reliable, and capable of delivering valuable insights.

4   AI IN EVERYDAY LIFE

4.1   SMART ASSISTANTS AND CHATBOTS

Artificial Intelligence (AI) has become deeply integrated into our daily lives, with smart   assistants and chatbots being two of the most prominent examples. These technologies leverage AI to enhance user convenience, provide assistance, and streamline various tasks. Here's an overview of how they work and their common applications:

4.1.1   SMART ASSISTANTS (HOW THEY WORK?)

- Voice Recognition:
  - ✓ Function: Smart assistants use voice recognition technology to understand spoken commands. This involves converting audio signals into text using Automatic Speech Recognition (ASR) algorithms.
  - ✓ Example: When you say, "Hey Siri" or "Okay Google," the assistant's microphone captures your voice, and ASR transcribes it into text.
- Natural Language Processing (NLP):
  - ✓ Function: NLP algorithms interpret the transcribed text to understand the meaning behind your commands. This involves parsing the text, identifying key phrases, and determining the intent.
  - ✓ Example: If you ask, "What's the weather today?" the assistant uses NLP to recognize that you're asking for weather information.
- Action Execution:
  - ✓ Function: Based on the interpreted command, the assistant performs the requested action or provides a response. This may involve accessing external data sources, interfacing with other apps, or controlling smart devices.
  - ✓ Example: The assistant might retrieve weather data from a weather service API and read it back to you.
- Machine Learning:
  - ✓ Function: Smart assistants use machine learning to improve their performance over time. They learn from user interactions, refine their language models, and adapt to individual preferences and speech patterns.
  - ✓ Example: Over time, the assistant might better understand your accent or recognize frequently asked questions more accurately.

4.1.2   SMART ASSISTANTS (COMMON APPLICATIONS)

- Personal Assistance:
  - ✓ Examples: Setting reminders, scheduling appointments, sending texts, and making phone calls. For instance, asking your assistant to "Set a reminder for 3 PM" or "Call Mom" are common uses.
- Information Retrieval:
  - ✓ Examples: Providing weather updates, news briefings, and general knowledge queries. Asking questions like "What's the latest news?" or "What's the capital of France?" falls into this category.
- Smart Home Control:

- ✓ Examples: Managing smart home devices like lights, thermostats, and security systems. Commands like "Turn off the lights" or "Set the thermostat to 72 degrees" are typical uses.
- Entertainment:
  - ✓ Examples: Playing music, podcasts, or audiobooks, and controlling streaming services. You might say, "Play jazz music" or "Play the latest episode of my favorite podcast."

4.1.3 CHATBOTS (HOW THEY WORK?)

- User Interaction:
  - ✓ Function: Chatbots engage users through text-based or voice-based conversations. They can be deployed on websites, messaging apps, or as standalone applications.
  - ✓ Example: A chatbot on a company's website might greet visitors and offer assistance with navigating the site or answering questions.
- Natural Language Understanding (NLU):
  - ✓ Function: NLU enables chatbots to interpret and understand user inputs. This involves analyzing text or voice inputs to extract meaningful information and determine user intent.
  - ✓ Example: If a user types "I need help with my order," the chatbot uses NLU to recognize that the user is seeking assistance with an order.
- Dialogue Management:
  - ✓ Function: Dialogue management systems maintain the flow of conversation by managing context and keeping track of the conversation history. This helps in generating coherent and contextually appropriate responses.
  - ✓ Example: The chatbot might remember previous interactions during the same session, such as an ongoing support ticket or product inquiry.
- Response Generation:
  - ✓ Function: Based on the user's intent and the context of the conversation, the chatbot generates appropriate responses. This can involve retrieving information from a knowledge base, executing predefined actions, or providing personalized replies.
  - ✓ Example: If a user asks, "What are your store hours?" the chatbot retrieves this information from its database and provides the response.
- Machine Learning and AI:
  - ✓ Function: Advanced chatbots use machine learning and AI to improve their conversational abilities over time. They learn from interactions, refine their responses, and handle more complex queries.
  - ✓ Example: A chatbot might improve its ability to handle customer complaints by analyzing feedback and adjusting its responses accordingly.

4.1.4 CHATBOTS (COMMON APPLICATIONS)

- Customer Support:
  - ✓ Examples: Assisting with common customer service inquiries, such as tracking orders, handling returns, and providing product information. For instance, a chatbot might help you track a shipment by asking for your order number.

- E-commerce:
  - ✓ Examples: Assisting users with product recommendations, helping with the purchase process, and answering product-related questions. A chatbot on an e-commerce site might suggest products based on browsing history or answer questions about shipping policies.
- Lead Generation:
  - ✓ Examples: Collecting user information and qualifying leads for sales teams. For example, a chatbot might ask users about their needs and collect contact information for follow-up.
- Booking and Reservations:
  - ✓ Examples: Facilitating bookings for hotels, restaurants, and events. A chatbot might assist you in booking a table at a restaurant or reserving a hotel room.

4.1.5 SUMMARY

Smart assistants and chatbots are powerful AI technologies that enhance everyday life by providing assistance, information, and automation. Smart assistants use voice recognition, natural language processing, and machine learning to perform a wide range of tasks, from managing personal schedules to controlling smart home devices. Chatbots, on the other hand, utilize natural language understanding and dialogue management to   engage users in text or voice conversations, assisting with customer support, e-commerce, and various other applications. Both technologies leverage AI to improve user experiences and streamline interactions, making daily tasks more convenient and efficient.

4.2   RECOMMENDATION SYSTEMS

Recommendation systems are AI-driven tools that provide personalized suggestions to users based on their preferences, behaviors, and interactions. These systems   play a crucial role in enhancing user experience by offering tailored content or products, helping users discover new items they might enjoy. Here's a look at how recommendation systems work and some examples in streaming services and online shopping:

4.2.1 HOW RECOMMENDATION SYSTEMS WORK

- Data Collection:
  - ✓ User Behavior: Collects data on user interactions, such as browsing history, clicks, ratings, and purchase history.
  - ✓ Item Features: Gathers information about the items themselves, such as product attributes, genres, or content descriptions.
  - ✓ User Profiles: Creates profiles based on user preferences, past interactions, and demographic information.
- Recommendation Algorithms:
  - ✓ Collaborative Filtering:
    - o User-Based: Suggests items based on the preferences of similar users. If User A and User B have similar tastes, the system might recommend items that User B liked to User A.

- o Item-Based: Recommends items similar to those the user has liked or interacted with before. If a user liked a specific movie, the system might suggest other movies with similar genres or actors.
  - ✓ Content-Based Filtering: Recommends items based on the features of the items themselves. For example, if a user enjoys action movies, the system will suggest other action movies based on their genre and characteristics.
  - ✓ Hybrid Methods: Combines collaborative filtering and content-based filtering to improve recommendation accuracy and address the limitations of each method.
- Personalization:
  - ✓ Real-Time Updates: Continuously updates recommendations based on new user interactions and feedback.
  - ✓ Contextual Factors: Considers contextual factors such as location, time of day, and recent activities to make more relevant suggestions.

4.2.2 EXAMPLES IN STREAMING SERVICES

- Netflix:
  - ✓ How It Works: Netflix uses a sophisticated recommendation system that combines collaborative filtering, content-based filtering, and deep learning algorithms. It analyzes users' viewing history, ratings, and search queries to suggest TV shows and movies.
  - ✓ Example: If you frequently watch science fiction films and rate them highly, Netflix will recommend other science fiction content that aligns with your preferences. It also considers factors such as viewing patterns and trends in similar user profiles.
- Spotify:
  - ✓ How It Works: Spotify's recommendation system leverages collaborative filtering, content-based filtering, and natural language processing to curate personalized playlists and music suggestions. It examines listening history, song preferences, and even lyrics analysis to provide recommendations.
  - ✓ Example: If you listen to a lot of indie rock music, Spotify's algorithm will suggest new indie rock tracks and artists, and create playlists like "Discover Weekly" tailored to your musical tastes.
- YouTube:
  - ✓ How It Works: YouTube uses a combination of collaborative filtering, content analysis, and deep learning to recommend videos. It looks at your watch history, search queries, and engagement metrics (likes, comments) to suggest videos you might find interesting.
  - ✓ Example: If you watch and like cooking tutorials, YouTube will recommend other cooking videos, channels, and related content based on your preferences and viewing habits.

4.2.3 EXAMPLES IN ONLINE SHOPPING

- Amazon:
  - ✓ How It Works: Amazon's recommendation system uses collaborative filtering, item-based recommendations, and content analysis to suggest

products. It examines your browsing history, past purchases, and the behavior of similar customers to make recommendations.
- ✓ Example: If you frequently purchase electronics, Amazon will suggest related products like accessories or complementary items. It also shows "Customers who bought this also bought" recommendations based on other users' purchase patterns.
- eBay:
  - ✓ How It Works: eBay employs collaborative filtering and content-based methods to recommend products. It uses data from your searches, watched items, and purchase history to suggest relevant listings.
  - ✓ Example: If you have shown interest in vintage collectibles, eBay will recommend similar vintage items and notify you of new listings that match your interests.
- Alibaba:
  - ✓ How It Works: Alibaba's recommendation system uses a mix of collaborative filtering, content-based filtering, and machine learning to suggest products to users. It takes into account users' browsing behavior, purchase history, and search queries.
  - ✓ Example: If you regularly search for beauty products, Alibaba will recommend related items such as new skincare products, beauty tools, and trending items based on your preferences.

4.2.4   SUMMARY

Recommendation systems are integral to many modern digital experiences, enhancing user satisfaction by providing personalized suggestions. In streaming services like Netflix, Spotify, and YouTube, recommendation systems help users discover new content based on their viewing and listening habits. In online shopping platforms like Amazon, eBay, and Alibaba, these systems suggest products based on user behavior and preferences. By leveraging data and sophisticated algorithms, recommendation systems play a crucial role in improving user engagement and satisfaction across various domains.

4.3   AI IN HEALTHCARE

Artificial Intelligence (AI) is revolutionizing healthcare by enhancing diagnostic capabilities and enabling more personalized treatment options. The integration of AI technologies into healthcare systems aims to improve patient outcomes, increase efficiency, and provide more targeted and effective treatments. Here's a closer look at how AI is transforming diagnostic tools and personalized medicine:

4.3.1   DIAGNOSTIC TOOLS (MEDICAL IMAGING ANALYSIS)

- Function:
  - ✓ AI Algorithms: AI algorithms, especially deep learning models, are used to analyze medical images such as X-rays, MRIs, and CT scans. These models can detect patterns and anomalies that might be missed by human eyes.
  - ✓ Examples: AI can identify tumors, fractures, or other abnormalities in medical images with high accuracy, assisting radiologists in making diagnoses.

- How It Works:
  - ✓ Image Processing: AI systems process and analyze vast amounts of image data. Convolutional Neural Networks (CNNs) are often employed to recognize and classify features in medical images.
  - ✓ Training: These models are trained on large datasets of annotated images to learn the characteristics of different conditions and improve their diagnostic accuracy.
- Benefits:
  - ✓ Early Detection: AI can help detect diseases at an earlier stage, improving the chances of successful treatment.
  - ✓ Consistency: AI systems provide consistent results, reducing variability and human error in diagnostic processes.
- Examples:
  - ✓ PathAI: Uses AI to analyze pathology slides and identify cancerous cells.
  - ✓ Google Health's AI for Retinal Disease: Detects signs of diabetic retinopathy and macular edema in retinal images.

4.3.2 PREDICTIVE ANALYTICS FOR DISEASE RISK

- Function:
  - ✓ Risk Assessment: AI models analyze patient data to predict the likelihood of developing certain diseases based on factors like medical history, genetics, and lifestyle.
  - ✓ Examples: Predictive models can forecast the risk of chronic diseases such as diabetes or heart disease.
- How It Works:
  - ✓ Data Integration: AI integrates data from electronic health records (EHRs), genetic information, and lifestyle factors.
  - ✓ Machine Learning: Machine learning algorithms analyze this data to identify patterns and correlations associated with disease risk.
- Benefits:
  - ✓ Proactive Care: Enables early interventions and preventive measures to manage or reduce the risk of developing diseases.
  - ✓ Tailored Recommendations: Provides personalized health recommendations based on individual risk profiles.
- Examples:
  - ✓ IBM Watson for Oncology: Analyzes patient data and medical literature to assist oncologists in predicting cancer treatment outcomes.
  - ✓ Cardiogram: Uses wearable device data to predict heart disease risk by analyzing heart rate patterns and other metrics.

4.3.3 PERSONALIZED MEDICINE (TAILORED TREATMENT PLANS)

- Function:
  - ✓ Customized Therapies: AI analyzes genetic, molecular, and clinical data to create personalized treatment plans that are more effective for individual patients.
  - ✓ Examples: AI helps in selecting the most appropriate drug or therapy based on a patient's unique genetic profile.

- How It Works:
  - ✓ Genomic Analysis: AI processes genomic data to identify genetic mutations and variations that influence drug responses and disease susceptibility.
  - ✓ Data Integration: Combines genetic data with clinical information to tailor treatment plans and predict responses to specific therapies.
- Benefits:
  - ✓ Increased Efficacy: Personalized treatments are more likely to be effective, reducing trial-and-error approaches and adverse reactions.
  - ✓ Optimized Outcomes: Enhances treatment outcomes by targeting therapies that align with the patient's genetic and molecular profile.
- Examples:
  - ✓ Foundation Medicine: Provides comprehensive genomic profiling to guide personalized cancer treatment options.
  - ✓ Tempus: Utilizes AI to analyze clinical and molecular data to help physicians make personalized treatment decisions for cancer patients.

4.3.4 DRUG DISCOVERY AND DEVELOPMENT

- Function:
  - ✓ Accelerated Discovery: AI accelerates the drug discovery process by analyzing vast amounts of biological data to identify potential drug candidates and predict their effectiveness.
  - ✓ Examples: AI can identify new drug targets, optimize drug formulations, and predict adverse effects before clinical trials.
- How It Works:
  - ✓ Data Analysis: AI systems analyze biological data, such as protein interactions and genetic information, to identify promising drug compounds and therapeutic targets.
  - ✓ Predictive Models: Machine learning models predict how different compounds interact with biological systems and their potential efficacy.
- Benefits:
  - ✓ Reduced Time and Cost: Speeds up the drug discovery process and reduces the costs associated with bringing new drugs to market.
  - ✓ Improved Accuracy: Enhances the accuracy of predictions about drug efficacy and safety, leading to more successful clinical trials.
- Examples:
  - ✓ DeepMind's AlphaFold: Uses AI to predict protein folding and structure, which is crucial for drug discovery and development.
  - ✓ BenevolentAI: Applies AI to analyze scientific literature and patient data to discover new drug candidates and repurpose existing drugs.

4.3.5 SUMMARY

AI is making significant strides in healthcare by enhancing diagnostic tools and enabling personalized medicine. In diagnostics, AI-driven tools such as medical imaging analysis and predictive analytics help in early disease detection and risk assessment. In personalized medicine, AI tailors treatment plans based on individual genetic and molecular profiles and accelerates drug discovery and development. By leveraging AI, healthcare providers can offer more accurate, efficient, and personalized care, ultimately leading to better patient outcomes and a more effective healthcare system.

4.4 AUTONOMOUS VEHICLES

Autonomous vehicles, commonly known as self-driving cars, represent a major leap in automotive technology. They use a combination of sensors, artificial intelligence (AI), and sophisticated algorithms to navigate and drive without human intervention. Here's a basic overview of how self-driving technology works:

4.4.1 SENSORS AND HARDWARE

- LiDAR (Light Detection and Ranging):
  - ✓ Function: LiDAR uses laser beams to create a 3D map of the vehicle's surroundings. It measures distances by calculating the time it takes for the laser to bounce back from objects.
  - ✓ Example: LiDAR helps the vehicle detect and map obstacles, road edges, and other objects with high precision.
- Cameras:
  - ✓ Function: Cameras capture visual information about the environment, such as lane markings, traffic signs, and other vehicles. They provide a comprehensive view of the surroundings.
  - ✓ Example: Cameras help in recognizing traffic lights, reading road signs, and detecting pedestrians.
- Radar (Radio Detection and Ranging):
  - ✓ Function: Radar uses radio waves to detect objects and measure their distance and speed. It works well in various weather conditions and can track moving objects.
  - ✓ Example: Radar is used for adaptive cruise control and collision avoidance by tracking the speed and distance of vehicles ahead.
- Ultrasonic Sensors:
  - ✓ Function: Ultrasonic sensors use sound waves to detect objects close to the vehicle, such as during parking maneuvers.
  - ✓ Example: These sensors help with parking assistance by detecting nearby obstacles and providing proximity warnings.

4.4.2 PERCEPTION SYSTEMS

- Object Detection:
  - ✓ Function: AI algorithms analyze data from sensors and cameras to identify and classify objects around the vehicle, such as other cars, pedestrians, cyclists, and obstacles.
  - ✓ Example: The system recognizes a pedestrian crossing the street and makes decisions to stop or navigate around them.
- Localization:
  - ✓ Function: The vehicle determines its precise location on the map using GPS, sensor data, and high-definition maps.
  - ✓ Example: Accurate localization allows the vehicle to follow the road and stay within its lane, even in complex environments.

- Mapping:
  - ✓ Function: High-definition maps provide detailed information about road features, traffic signals, and other infrastructure. These maps are used to plan routes and navigate accurately.
  - ✓ Example: Maps include information about road curvature, lane markings, and traffic signal locations to assist in route planning and safe driving.

4.4.3 DECISION-MAKING AND CONTROL

- Path Planning:
  - ✓ Function: AI algorithms plan the vehicle's path by considering current conditions, obstacles, and traffic rules. The system determines the best route and maneuvers to reach the destination safely.
  - ✓ Example: Path planning involves calculating lane changes, turns, and speed adjustments based on the vehicle's surroundings and destination.
- Control Systems:
  - ✓ Function: Control systems manage the vehicle's steering, acceleration, and braking based on the planned path and real-time data from sensors.
  - ✓ Example: The system adjusts steering to keep the vehicle in the center of the lane, applies brakes to slow down, and accelerates to maintain the desired speed.
- Behavior Prediction:
  - ✓ Function: AI models predict the behavior of other road users, such as other vehicles, pedestrians, and cyclists. This helps in making proactive decisions and avoiding potential collisions.
  - ✓ Example: The system anticipates that a car in the adjacent lane might merge into the current lane and adjusts the vehicle's speed and position accordingly.

4.4.4 MACHINE LEARNING AND AI

- Training Algorithms:
  - ✓ Function: AI models are trained using large datasets of driving scenarios, including various traffic situations, road conditions, and driving behaviors.
  - ✓ Example: Machine learning algorithms learn from thousands of hours of driving data to recognize patterns, improve decision-making, and enhance safety.
- Continuous Learning:
  - ✓ Function: Autonomous vehicles continuously learn and improve their performance based on new data collected during operation. This allows them to adapt to changing environments and driving conditions.
  - ✓ Example: The system updates its models to handle new types of road signs or unusual driving situations more effectively.

4.4.5 LEVELS OF AUTONOMY

Autonomous vehicles are categorized into different levels based on their degree of automation, as defined by the Society of Automotive Engineers (SAE):

- Level 0 (No Automation): The human driver performs all driving tasks.

- Level 1 (Driver Assistance): Basic assistance with features like adaptive cruise control or lane-keeping, but the driver remains responsible for all driving tasks.
- Level 2 (Partial Automation): The vehicle can control both steering and acceleration, but the driver must monitor the environment and be ready to take over.
- Level 3 (Conditional Automation): The vehicle can handle all driving tasks under certain conditions, but the driver must be available to take over when requested.
- Level 4 (High Automation): The vehicle can operate autonomously in specific conditions or geofenced areas, with no driver intervention needed.
- Level 5 (Full Automation): The vehicle is fully autonomous and can operate in all conditions without any human input.

4.4.6   SUMMARY

Self-driving technology combines advanced sensors, AI algorithms, and machine learning to create autonomous vehicles capable of navigating and driving without human intervention. Core technologies include LiDAR, cameras, radar, and ultrasonic sensors, which provide the necessary data for perception and decision-making systems. Autonomous vehicles use these systems to plan paths, control driving actions, and predict the behavior of other road users. With various levels of automation, from basic driver assistance to full autonomy, self-driving technology is advancing towards making safer, more efficient, and fully autonomous transportation a reality.

5 THE POWER AND LIMITATIONS OF AI

5.1 STRENGTHS OF AI

Artificial Intelligence (AI) has emerged as a transformative technology, significantly impacting various domains from healthcare to finance and beyond. Its strengths lie in its ability to handle complex tasks with remarkable efficiency, scalability, and pattern recognition capabilities. Here's an overview of these key strengths:

5.1.1 EFFICIENCY

- Speed and Automation:
  - ✓ Function: AI systems can process and analyze data at speeds far beyond human capabilities. This efficiency is crucial for tasks that require handling large volumes of information quickly and accurately.
  - ✓ Examples:
    - o Data Processing: AI can analyze massive datasets, such as customer interactions or financial transactions, in real time. This capability is essential for applications like fraud detection and real-time recommendation systems.
    - o Automated Workflows: AI automates repetitive tasks such as data entry, customer support responses, and scheduling. For example, chatbots can handle thousands of customer inquiries simultaneously, reducing the need for human intervention.
- Precision and Accuracy:
  - ✓ Function: AI algorithms perform tasks with high precision, reducing errors and inconsistencies that might occur with manual processes.
  - ✓ Examples:
    - o Medical Diagnostics: AI-powered diagnostic tools analyze medical images to detect abnormalities with high accuracy, often surpassing human radiologists in certain areas.
    - o Manufacturing: AI-driven robots and systems in manufacturing ensure consistent quality and precision in production lines, minimizing defects and waste.

5.1.2 SCALABILITY

- Handling Large Volumes of Data:
  - ✓ Function: AI systems can scale to handle vast amounts of data, making them well-suited for applications that involve big data.
  - ✓ Examples:
    - o Search Engines: AI algorithms in search engines like Google process and index billions of web pages to deliver relevant search results quickly.
    - o Social Media Platforms: AI analyzes user interactions, posts, and trends across millions of users to provide personalized content and advertisements.
- Adaptability to Growth:
  - ✓ Function: AI systems can be scaled up or down based on demand, making them adaptable to growing needs without significant reengineering.

✓ Examples:
  o Cloud Computing: AI applications deployed in the cloud can easily adjust resources based on usage, allowing for flexible scaling as user demand increases.
  o E-commerce: AI-driven recommendation engines can scale to handle increasing numbers of products and users, continuously providing personalized suggestions.

5.1.3 PATTERN RECOGNITION

- Identifying Trends and Insights:
  ✓ Function: AI excels at recognizing patterns and trends in data that may be subtle or complex for humans to detect.
  ✓ Examples:
    o Financial Markets: AI models analyze historical market data to identify trading patterns, trends, and potential investment opportunities.
    o Healthcare: AI identifies patterns in patient data, such as symptoms and genetic information, to predict disease outbreaks or patient outcomes.
- Predictive Analytics:
  ✓ Function: AI can forecast future trends and behaviors by analyzing historical data and identifying patterns.
  ✓ Examples:
    o Retail: AI predicts customer purchasing behavior, inventory needs, and market demand, helping businesses optimize stock levels and marketing strategies.
    o Weather Forecasting: AI models analyze meteorological data to predict weather patterns and extreme weather events with high accuracy.
- Image and Speech Recognition:
  ✓ Function: AI systems use pattern recognition to interpret and understand images and spoken language, enabling various applications.
  ✓ Examples:
    o Facial Recognition: AI algorithms identify and verify individuals based on facial features, used in security systems and social media tagging.
    o Voice Assistants: AI-powered voice recognition systems understand and respond to spoken commands, enabling hands-free control of devices.

5.1.4 SUMMARY

AI's strengths lie in its efficiency, scalability, and pattern recognition capabilities. It can process and analyze data with high speed and accuracy, automate repetitive tasks, and scale to handle large volumes of information. Its ability to recognize complex patterns enables it to provide valuable insights and predictions across various domains. These strengths make AI a powerful tool in driving innovation and enhancing productivity, although it's important to also consider its limitations and challenges in the broader context.

5.2   LIMITATIONS AND CHALLENGES

While AI offers remarkable strengths in efficiency, scalability, and pattern recognition, it also faces significant limitations and challenges. These include issues related to bias, data quality, and ethical concerns. Understanding these challenges is crucial for developing and deploying AI systems responsibly.

5.2.1   BIAS

- Sources of Bias:
  - ✓ Training Data Bias:
    - o Function: AI systems learn from historical data, which may contain inherent biases reflecting historical inequalities or prejudices. These biases can be inadvertently encoded into the AI models.
    - o Examples: If an AI model is trained on data from a particular demographic group, it may perform less accurately for individuals from different groups.
  - ✓ Algorithmic Bias:
    - o Function: Biases in the design or implementation of algorithms can lead to skewed outcomes. The algorithms themselves may amplify existing biases present in the data.
    - o Examples: An algorithm used for hiring might favor candidates with specific educational backgrounds, inadvertently discriminating against equally qualified candidates from diverse backgrounds.
- Implications of Bias:
  - ✓ Discrimination:
    - o Function: AI systems can perpetuate or even exacerbate existing social biases, leading to unfair treatment of individuals based on race, gender, age, or other characteristics.
    - o Examples: AI in criminal justice systems might disproportionately target certain racial groups, while facial recognition systems might have higher error rates for minority groups.
  - ✓ Trust and Acceptance:
    - o Function: Bias in AI can erode public trust in technology and its applications, affecting user acceptance and the perceived fairness of AI systems.
    - o Examples: If users experience biased recommendations or unfair treatment, they may become skeptical of AI technologies and their benefits.
- Mitigation Strategies:
  - ✓ Diverse Data:
    - o Function: Ensuring that training data is diverse and representative of different groups can help reduce bias.
    - o Examples: Collecting data from various demographics and scenarios to train models can improve fairness and accuracy.
  - ✓ Bias Detection and Correction:
    - o Function: Implementing methods to detect and correct biases in AI models, such as fairness audits and algorithmic adjustments.

- o Examples: Regularly testing models for biased outcomes and adjusting algorithms to mitigate identified biases.

5.2.2 DATA QUALITY

- Importance of Data Quality:
  - ✓ Accuracy and Completeness:
    - o Function: High-quality data is essential for training accurate AI models. Inaccurate or incomplete data can lead to incorrect predictions and unreliable results.
    - o Examples: Medical AI systems relying on flawed data might misdiagnose conditions or provide incorrect treatment recommendations.
  - ✓ Relevance and Currency:
    - o Function: Data used for training must be relevant and up-to-date to ensure that AI systems make decisions based on current trends and information.
    - o Examples: An AI model for financial forecasting needs recent market data to provide accurate predictions, while outdated data could lead to poor investment decisions.
- Challenges with Data Quality:
  - ✓ Data Collection:
    - o Function: Collecting and curating high-quality data can be time-consuming, expensive, and challenging, especially for niche applications.
    - o Examples: Gathering comprehensive and accurate medical records for training healthcare AI can be difficult due to privacy concerns and data availability.
  - ✓ Data Privacy and Security:
    - o Function: Ensuring the privacy and security of data is crucial, as breaches or misuse of data can compromise both individuals and systems.
    - o Examples: Personal data used in AI systems must be protected to prevent unauthorized access and potential misuse, such as identity theft or unauthorized profiling.
- Improvement Strategies:
  - ✓ Data Cleaning:
    - o Function: Regularly cleaning and validating data to remove errors and inconsistencies.
    - o Examples: Implementing processes to identify and correct data inaccuracies or gaps before using it for training AI models.
  - ✓ Data Governance:
    - o Function: Establishing robust data governance practices to ensure data quality, security, and compliance with regulations.
    - o Examples: Adopting policies for data management, privacy protection, and security to maintain high standards of data integrity.

5.2.3 ETHICAL CONCERNS

- Transparency and Accountability:
  - ✓ Function: AI systems often operate as "black boxes," where their decision-making processes are not easily understood. Ensuring transparency and accountability is crucial for trust and ethical use.

    ✓ Examples: Users and stakeholders should be able to understand how AI systems make decisions and hold developers accountable for their outcomes.

- Privacy and Surveillance:
  - ✓ Function: AI technologies, especially those involving personal data, raise concerns about privacy and surveillance. Balancing the benefits of AI with the need for privacy is essential.
  - ✓ Examples: AI-powered surveillance systems can track individuals' activities, raising concerns about intrusive monitoring and loss of personal privacy.
- Ethical Use and Misuse:
  - ✓ Function: Ensuring that AI is used ethically and not for harmful purposes, such as manipulation, discrimination, or unintended consequences.
  - ✓ Examples: AI-generated deepfakes can be used to spread misinformation, while biased algorithms might reinforce social inequalities.
- Regulation and Policy:
  - ✓ Function: Developing and implementing regulations and policies to guide the ethical development and use of AI technologies.
  - ✓ Examples: Governments and organizations are working to create frameworks for responsible AI use, including ethical guidelines, standards for transparency, and protections for individuals' rights.

5.2.4   SUMMARY

AI's limitations and challenges, including bias, data quality issues, and ethical concerns, highlight the need for careful consideration and management. Addressing these challenges involves ensuring diverse and high-quality data, detecting and mitigating biases, and adhering to ethical standards and regulations. By tackling these issues, we can harness the benefits of AI while minimizing potential risks and ensuring that AI technologies are used responsibly and fairly.

6 ETHICAL AND SOCIETAL IMPLICATIONS

6.1 AI AND PRIVACY

As AI technology becomes more integrated into daily life, issues surrounding data privacy and security have become increasingly important. AI systems rely heavily on data to function effectively, but this reliance raises significant concerns about how personal information is collected, used, and protected. Here's a detailed look at the key privacy and security concerns related to AI:

6.1.1 DATA PRIVACY CONCERNS

- Data Collection and Consent
  - ✓ Function: AI systems often require large amounts of data to train and operate effectively. This data can include personal information such as browsing history, medical records, and location data.
  - ✓ Concerns:
    - o Informed Consent: Users may not always be fully aware of what data is being collected or how it will be used. Informed consent requires transparency about data practices and obtaining explicit permission from users.
    - o Data Ownership: Questions about who owns and controls personal data arise. Users often have limited control over how their data is used once it is collected by AI systems.
  - ✓ Examples:
    - o Social Media Platforms: Platforms collect extensive data on user behavior, interactions, and preferences, which may be used for targeted advertising or other purposes without clear consent.
    - o Health Apps: Apps that track personal health information may share data with third parties, raising concerns about how this sensitive information is managed and protected.
- Data Usage and Profiling
  - ✓ Function: AI systems use collected data to create detailed profiles of individuals, which can be used for targeted advertising, personalized recommendations, or even decision-making in critical areas like credit scoring.
  - ✓ Concerns:
    - o Privacy Invasion: Detailed profiling can lead to intrusive practices, where users' behavior and preferences are analyzed in ways they may find uncomfortable or invasive.
    - o Discrimination: Profiling can result in discriminatory practices, such as biased decision-making in hiring or loan approvals based on inaccurate or unfair assessments.
  - ✓ Examples:
    - o Advertising: AI algorithms create detailed user profiles to deliver targeted ads, which can sometimes feel overly invasive or manipulative.
    - o Insurance: AI-driven risk assessments might lead to higher premiums for individuals based on predictive models, potentially reinforcing existing inequalities.

- Data Retention and Disposal
  - ✓ Function: AI systems often store large amounts of personal data over extended periods. Proper management of data retention and disposal is crucial to protecting user privacy.
  - ✓ Concerns:
    - o Data Breaches: Long-term storage increases the risk of data breaches. Stolen data can be used maliciously, compromising user privacy.
    - o Data Deletion: Ensuring that data is properly deleted when it is no longer needed or when a user requests deletion is essential for protecting privacy.
  - ✓ Examples:
    - o Data Breaches: High-profile breaches, such as those involving personal information from major corporations, highlight the risks associated with inadequate data protection practices.
    - o Retention Policies: Companies must implement clear policies for data retention and deletion to comply with regulations and protect user privacy.

6.1.2   SECURITY CONCERNS

- Data Security
  - ✓ Function: AI systems process sensitive and valuable data, which must be securely stored and transmitted to prevent unauthorized access and misuse.
  - ✓ Concerns:
    - o Cyberattacks: AI systems can be targeted by cyberattacks, including data breaches and ransomware, which can compromise personal information and system integrity.
    - o Vulnerabilities: AI systems themselves may have vulnerabilities that can be exploited by attackers, potentially leading to unauthorized access or manipulation of data.
  - ✓ Examples:
    - o Ransomware Attacks: Cybercriminals may target AI systems with ransomware, locking access to critical data until a ransom is paid.
    - o Data Manipulation: Attackers might manipulate AI models by injecting malicious data, leading to incorrect predictions or decisions.
- Security of AI Systems
  - ✓ Function: Ensuring the security of the AI systems themselves is critical to protecting the data they handle and maintaining trust in their operations.
  - ✓ Concerns:
    - o Adversarial Attacks: AI models can be vulnerable to adversarial attacks, where attackers input carefully crafted data to deceive or mislead the system.
    - o Model Integrity: Protecting the integrity of AI models is essential to prevent tampering or unauthorized modifications that could lead to harmful outcomes.
  - ✓ Examples:
    - o Adversarial Examples: Techniques such as adding subtle noise to inputs can trick AI systems into making incorrect classifications or decisions.
    - o Model Theft: AI models, especially those developed with significant investment, can be targeted for theft, potentially leading to intellectual property loss and security risks.

- Compliance with Regulations
  - ✓ Function: Adhering to data protection regulations is essential for ensuring that AI systems operate within legal and ethical boundaries.
  - ✓ Concerns:
    - o Regulatory Compliance: AI systems must comply with regulations such as the General Data Protection Regulation (GDPR) in Europe or the California Consumer Privacy Act (CCPA) in the U.S., which govern data collection, usage, and protection.
    - o Enforcement: Ensuring that AI systems comply with regulations and that violations are addressed can be challenging, requiring robust oversight and enforcement mechanisms.
  - ✓ Examples:
    - o GDPR Compliance: Organizations must ensure that their AI systems comply with GDPR requirements for data protection, including providing users with access to their data and the ability to request deletion.
    - o CCPA Compliance: AI systems operating in California must adhere to CCPA regulations, which grant users rights related to their personal data and require transparency in data practices.

6.1.3 SUMMARY

AI's impact on privacy and security brings both opportunities and challenges. Data privacy issues include concerns about consent, ownership, and the potential for invasive profiling. Security concerns focus on the risks of cyberattacks, data breaches, and the need for robust protection of AI systems and data. Addressing these concerns involves implementing strong data protection practices, ensuring compliance with regulations, and developing AI systems that respect user privacy and security. By navigating these challenges carefully, we can leverage AI's benefits while safeguarding individual rights and maintaining trust.

6.2 BIAS AND FAIRNESS

Bias in AI can have profound effects on outcomes and decision-making processes. Understanding how bias impacts AI and exploring solutions to mitigate it are crucial for developing fair and equitable systems. Here's a detailed look at the influence of bias on AI and potential strategies for addressing it:

6.2.1 HOW BIAS AFFECTS AI OUTCOMES

- Discrimination and Inequality
  - ✓ Function: Bias in AI can lead to discriminatory practices, where certain groups are unfairly treated or disadvantaged based on race, gender, age, or other characteristics.
  - ✓ Examples:
    - o Hiring Algorithms: AI systems used in recruitment may unintentionally favor candidates from certain backgrounds, leading to unequal opportunities for applicants from underrepresented groups.

- o Credit Scoring: Algorithms used for credit assessments might disproportionately affect individuals from marginalized communities, potentially leading to unfair lending practices.
- Accuracy and Reliability
  - ✓ Function: Bias can reduce the accuracy and reliability of AI systems by skewing results and predictions. This can lead to erroneous or unfair outcomes.
  - ✓ Examples:
    - o Facial Recognition: AI systems trained on limited or unrepresentative datasets may have higher error rates for minority groups, leading to misidentifications or failures in recognition.
    - o Medical Diagnostics: Bias in training data can affect the accuracy of diagnostic tools, potentially leading to incorrect or suboptimal healthcare recommendations for certain populations.
- Trust and Acceptance
  - ✓ Function: Bias can undermine public trust in AI systems. If users perceive that AI decisions are unfair or biased, they may be less likely to accept or use these technologies.
  - ✓ Examples:
    - o Customer Service: AI chatbots that provide biased responses or recommendations can lead to dissatisfaction and loss of trust among users.
    - o Law Enforcement: AI tools used in policing or legal contexts that exhibit bias can erode trust in the justice system and contribute to social inequality.
- Legal and Ethical Implications
  - ✓ Function: Biased AI outcomes can lead to legal and ethical challenges, including violations of anti-discrimination laws and ethical principles.
  - ✓ Examples:
    - o Legal Actions: Organizations may face lawsuits or regulatory actions if their AI systems are found to discriminate against certain groups.
    - o Ethical Dilemmas: Ethical concerns arise when AI systems perpetuate or amplify existing social biases, raising questions about fairness and justice.

6.2.2   SOLUTIONS TO ADDRESS BIAS

- Diverse and Representative Data
  - ✓ Function: Using diverse and representative datasets can help mitigate bias by ensuring that AI systems are trained on data that reflects various demographics and scenarios.
  - ✓ Strategies:
    - o Inclusive Data Collection: Gather data from a wide range of sources and demographics to ensure that all relevant groups are represented.
    - o Bias Audits: Regularly audit datasets for biases and imbalances, and adjust data collection practices to address identified issues.
  - ✓ Examples:
    - o Medical Research: Ensuring that clinical trials include participants from diverse backgrounds to create more inclusive medical AI models.
    - o Recruitment Tools: Training hiring algorithms on diverse candidate pools to reduce bias in candidate selection.

- Fairness-Enhancing Algorithms
  - ✓ Function: Implementing fairness-enhancing algorithms and techniques can help reduce bias in AI models and promote equitable outcomes.
  - ✓ Strategies:
    - o Bias Mitigation Algorithms: Use algorithms designed to detect and correct biases in predictions or classifications.
    - o Fairness Constraints: Incorporate fairness constraints into model training to ensure that outcomes are equitable across different groups.
  - ✓ Examples:
    - o Re-weighting Techniques: Adjusting the importance of different data points to balance the impact of underrepresented groups in model training.
    - o Fairness Metrics: Evaluating AI models using fairness metrics to ensure that they provide equitable results.
- Transparent and Explainable AI
  - ✓ Function: Enhancing the transparency and explainability of AI systems can help identify and address biases, and build trust with users.
  - ✓ Strategies:
    - o Model Interpretability: Develop AI models that provide clear explanations of their decisions and predictions.
    - o Transparency Reports: Publish transparency reports detailing data sources, model development processes, and fairness evaluations.
  - ✓ Examples:
    - o Explainable AI Tools: Using tools and techniques that make AI decision-making processes more understandable to users and stakeholders.
    - o Public Reporting: Providing detailed information about how AI systems are developed and evaluated to promote accountability.
- Ethical and Inclusive Design Practices
  - ✓ Function: Adopting ethical and inclusive design practices ensures that AI systems are developed with fairness and equity in mind.
  - ✓ Strategies:
    - o Ethical Guidelines: Follow ethical guidelines and best practices for AI development, including considerations for fairness and inclusivity.
    - o Stakeholder Involvement: Engage diverse stakeholders in the design and evaluation of AI systems to gather different perspectives and address potential biases.
  - ✓ Examples:
    - o Ethical Reviews: Conducting ethical reviews and impact assessments during the AI development process to identify and address potential biases.
    - o Inclusive Teams: Assembling diverse teams of developers, researchers, and stakeholders to ensure that various perspectives are considered in AI design.
- Ongoing Monitoring and Feedback
  - ✓ Function: Continuously monitoring AI systems and incorporating user feedback helps identify and address emerging biases over time.
  - ✓ Strategies:
    - o Regular Audits: Conduct regular audits and evaluations of AI systems to assess their performance and fairness.

- o User Feedback: Collect and incorporate feedback from users to address any concerns about bias and improve system performance.
- ✓ Examples:
  - o Performance Reviews: Regularly reviewing AI system performance to detect and correct any biased outcomes.
  - o Feedback Mechanisms: Implementing mechanisms for users to report and address issues related to bias and fairness.

6.2.3 SUMMARY

Bias in AI can lead to discriminatory practices, reduced accuracy, and diminished trust in technology. Addressing these issues involves using diverse data, implementing fairness-enhancing algorithms, and ensuring transparency and ethical design. By proactively addressing bias and incorporating inclusive practices, we can develop AI systems that promote fairness and equitable outcomes for all users.

6.3 JOB DISPLACEMENT AND ECONOMIC IMPACT

The advent of artificial intelligence (AI) brings transformative potential but also raises concerns about job displacement and economic shifts. As AI technologies evolve and integrate into various industries, their impact on employment and the broader economy becomes increasingly significant. Here's a detailed look at the potential effects of AI on jobs and economic structures:

6.3.1 POTENTIAL EFFECTS ON EMPLOYMENT

- Job Displacement
  - ✓ Function: AI and automation can replace certain types of jobs, particularly those involving repetitive or routine tasks. This displacement can affect workers across various sectors.
  - ✓ Examples:
    - o Manufacturing: Robots and automated systems can handle tasks such as assembly line work, reducing the need for manual labor in factories.
    - o Customer Service: AI-powered chatbots and virtual assistants can perform routine customer support tasks, potentially displacing human customer service representatives.
- Job Transformation
  - ✓ Function: While AI may displace some jobs, it also transforms existing roles by automating specific tasks, requiring workers to adapt and acquire new skills.
  - ✓ Examples:
    - o Healthcare: AI can assist with diagnostic tasks, allowing medical professionals to focus on more complex and personalized care.
    - o Finance: AI can automate data analysis and reporting, enabling financial analysts to concentrate on strategic decision-making and client interactions.
- Job Creation
  - ✓ Function: AI technology can create new job opportunities in emerging fields and industries, often requiring specialized skills and expertise.

- ✓ Examples:
  - o AI Development: Jobs related to developing, maintaining, and improving AI systems, including roles for data scientists, machine learning engineers, and AI researchers.
  - o AI Ethics and Regulation: New roles focused on ensuring ethical AI use, developing regulations, and addressing societal impacts of AI technologies.
- Skills and Education
  - ✓ Function: The rise of AI necessitates a shift in skills and education, emphasizing the need for continuous learning and adaptation to new technological demands.
  - ✓ Examples:
    - o Technical Skills: Increasing demand for skills in programming, data analysis, and AI system management.
    - o Soft Skills: Emphasis on critical thinking, problem-solving, and creativity, as these skills are less likely to be automated.

6.3.2 POTENTIAL ECONOMIC IMPACTS

- Productivity and Growth
  - ✓ Function: AI can significantly boost productivity by automating tasks, optimizing processes, and enabling more efficient use of resources, potentially leading to economic growth.
  - ✓ Examples:
    - o Business Efficiency: AI-driven automation can enhance operational efficiency in sectors like logistics, manufacturing, and retail, leading to cost savings and increased output.
    - o Innovation: AI fosters innovation by enabling new products and services, driving economic growth and creating new market opportunities.
- Income Inequality
  - ✓ Function: The benefits of AI may not be evenly distributed, potentially exacerbating income inequality. Workers in low-skill or routine jobs might face more significant challenges compared to those in high-skill or tech-focused roles.
  - ✓ Examples:
    - o Wage Disparities: Higher wages for jobs in AI development and technology sectors, while workers in automated roles may face wage stagnation or job loss.
    - o Regional Differences: Regions with strong technology sectors may benefit more from AI advancements compared to areas reliant on industries susceptible to automation.
- Economic Restructuring
  - ✓ Function: AI can drive economic restructuring as industries evolve and new sectors emerge, requiring adjustments in labor markets and economic policies.
  - ✓ Examples:
    - o Sector Shifts: Growth in technology and service sectors may offset declines in traditional manufacturing or administrative roles.

- o Policy Responses: Governments may need to develop policies to support displaced workers, promote reskilling, and ensure that economic benefits are broadly shared.
- ▪ Entrepreneurship and Startups
  - ✓ Function: AI technology can lower barriers to entry for entrepreneurship, enabling startups and small businesses to leverage AI for innovation and competitiveness.
  - ✓ Examples:
    - o Tech Startups: Entrepreneurs can create new AI-driven products and services, fostering innovation and contributing to economic dynamism.
    - o Small Business Tools: AI-powered tools can help small businesses streamline operations, manage customer relationships, and compete in the market.
- ▪ Social Safety Nets
  - ✓ Function: The economic impacts of AI may necessitate enhanced social safety nets and support systems to address the needs of displaced workers and affected communities.
  - ✓ Examples:
    - o Unemployment Benefits: Strengthening unemployment benefits and job retraining programs to support workers who lose their jobs due to automation.
    - o Universal Basic Income: Exploring concepts like universal basic income (UBI) to provide financial stability as the job market undergoes transformation.

6.3.3   SUMMARY

The integration of AI into the economy presents both opportunities and challenges. While AI can displace certain jobs and transform others, it also creates new roles and drives economic growth through increased productivity and innovation. Addressing the potential impacts of AI requires proactive measures, including reskilling programs, policies to manage income inequality, and support for displaced workers. By navigating these challenges thoughtfully, we can harness the benefits of AI while ensuring that its economic impact is equitable and beneficial for all.

7 THE FUTURE OF AI

7.1 EMERGING TRENDS AND TECHNOLOGIES

Artificial Intelligence (AI) continues to evolve at a rapid pace, with significant advancements in research and development shaping its future. These emerging trends and technologies promise to transform industries, enhance capabilities, and introduce new possibilities. Here's an overview of the key trends and technologies that are driving the future of AI:

7.1.1 ADVANCES IN AI RESEARCH AND DEVELOPMENT

- General AI and Superintelligence
  - ✓ Function: While current AI systems are generally narrow or specialized, research is ongoing to develop General AI (AGI) — AI systems with human-like cognitive abilities — and even Superintelligence, where AI surpasses human intelligence across all domains.
  - ✓ Trends:
    - o AGI Research: Scientists are exploring architectures and learning approaches that could enable machines to understand, learn, and apply knowledge in a more generalized way, similar to human cognition.
    - o Superintelligence: Research into superintelligent AI focuses on theoretical frameworks and safety measures to manage potential risks associated with AI far exceeding human intelligence.
  - ✓ Examples:
    - o OpenAI's GPT Models: Continued development towards more sophisticated language models that approach generalized understanding and reasoning capabilities.
    - o DeepMind's Research: Initiatives aiming at building AGI through advanced reinforcement learning and multi-task learning approaches.
- Improved Natural Language Processing (NLP)
  - ✓ Function: Advances in NLP are enabling AI systems to understand, generate, and interact with human language more effectively and naturally.
  - ✓ Trends:
    - o Conversational AI: Development of more advanced chatbots and virtual assistants that can engage in more meaningful and context-aware conversations.
    - o Language Understanding: Improvements in models for better understanding of context, intent, and nuance in human language.
  - ✓ Examples:
    - o Transformer Models: Continued refinement of transformer-based architectures (like BERT and GPT) that enhance language understanding and generation capabilities.
    - o Contextual AI: AI systems that can maintain context across longer conversations and understand subtleties in language.
- AI in Healthcare
  - ✓ Function: AI is making significant strides in healthcare, improving diagnostics, treatment planning, and personalized medicine.
  - ✓ Trends:

- o Precision Medicine: Development of AI systems for personalized treatment plans based on genetic, environmental, and lifestyle factors.
- o Predictive Analytics: AI tools for early detection of diseases through analysis of medical imaging and patient data.
  - ✓ Examples:
    - o AI Diagnostics: Tools like IBM Watson Health that analyze medical records and research to provide diagnostic and treatment recommendations.
    - o Genomic Data Analysis: AI models that assist in interpreting genetic information and tailoring treatments for individual patients.
- Autonomous Systems
  - ✓ Function: Advances in autonomous systems are leading to the development of self-driving vehicles, drones, and robots that can operate independently in complex environments.
  - ✓ Trends:
    - o Autonomous Vehicles: Progress in self-driving technology, including improved safety features, navigation systems, and integration with smart infrastructure.
    - o Drone Technology: Enhanced capabilities for drones in areas like delivery, surveillance, and environmental monitoring.
  - ✓ Examples:
    - o Waymo and Tesla: Ongoing advancements in autonomous driving technologies that aim to make self-driving cars safer and more efficient.
    - o Delivery Drones: Companies like Amazon and Google experimenting with drones for package delivery and logistical support.
- Edge AI
  - ✓ Function: Edge AI involves processing data locally on devices rather than sending it to centralized servers, reducing latency and improving real-time decision-making.
  - ✓ Trends:
    - o On-Device AI: Development of AI algorithms and models that run on edge devices like smartphones, IoT devices, and smart cameras.
    - o Real-Time Processing: Enhancement of real-time data processing capabilities for applications requiring low latency and high efficiency.
  - ✓ Examples:
    - o Smartphones: AI features such as facial recognition and voice assistants running directly on mobile devices.
    - o IoT Devices: Smart home devices and sensors that process data locally to enable quick responses and automation.
- AI Ethics and Governance
  - ✓ Function: As AI technologies advance, there is a growing emphasis on developing frameworks for ethical AI use, fairness, transparency, and accountability.
  - ✓ Trends:
    - o Ethical Guidelines: Creation of guidelines and standards to ensure AI systems are developed and used ethically.

- o Governance Frameworks: Development of regulatory and oversight mechanisms to manage AI's societal impacts and ensure compliance with ethical standards.
  - ✓ Examples:
    - o AI Ethics Boards: Establishment of ethics committees and boards within organizations to oversee AI development and deployment.
    - o Policy Initiatives: Governments and international bodies working on policies and regulations to guide the responsible use of AI technologies.
- Quantum Computing and AI
  - ✓ Function: Quantum computing holds the potential to revolutionize AI by solving complex problems that are currently beyond the capabilities of classical computers.
  - ✓ Trends:
    - o Quantum Algorithms: Development of quantum algorithms that could enhance machine learning and optimization tasks.
    - o Hybrid Systems: Exploration of hybrid quantum-classical systems that combine quantum computing's power with traditional AI techniques.
  - ✓ Examples:
    - o IBM's Quantum Computing: Efforts to integrate quantum computing with AI for advanced data analysis and problem-solving.
    - o Google's Quantum Supremacy: Demonstrations of quantum computing's potential to solve specific problems faster than classical computers.

7.1.2   SUMMARY

The future of AI is marked by rapid advancements across various domains, including the development of General AI, breakthroughs in natural language processing, and improvements in healthcare and autonomous systems. Emerging trends such as edge AI, quantum computing, and AI ethics are shaping the trajectory of AI technologies. As AI continues to evolve, balancing innovation with ethical considerations and governance will be crucial in ensuring that its benefits are maximized while addressing potential risks and challenges.

7.2   AI AND HUMAN COLLABORATION

Artificial Intelligence (AI) is not just about replacing human jobs; it's also about augmenting human abilities and fostering collaboration between humans and machines. By complementing human skills, AI can enhance productivity, creativity, and decision-making across various fields. Here's an overview of how AI can work alongside humans to create more effective and innovative outcomes:

7.2.1   ENHANCING DECISION-MAKING

- Data Analysis and Insights
  - ✓ Function: AI can process and analyze vast amounts of data far more quickly and accurately than humans, providing valuable insights that support better decision-making.
  - ✓ Examples:

- o Financial Services: AI algorithms analyze market trends and financial data to provide investment recommendations, aiding financial analysts in making informed decisions.
- o Healthcare: AI systems analyze patient data and medical research to support doctors in diagnosing diseases and selecting treatment plans.
- Predictive Analytics
  - ✓ Function: AI can predict future trends based on historical data, helping humans anticipate and prepare for potential outcomes.
  - ✓ Examples:
    - o Retail: AI-driven predictive analytics forecast customer demand and inventory needs, enabling retailers to optimize stock levels and reduce waste.
    - o Weather Forecasting: AI models improve the accuracy of weather predictions, aiding meteorologists in providing timely and precise forecasts.

7.2.2   AUGMENTING CREATIVITY

- Creative Collaboration
  - ✓ Function: AI tools can assist in creative processes by generating ideas, providing suggestions, and automating repetitive tasks, allowing humans to focus on higher-level creativity.
  - ✓ Examples:
    - o Art and Design: AI-powered tools can generate artwork, design elements, or music compositions, which artists and designers can then refine and adapt.
    - o Content Creation: AI can assist writers by suggesting topics, generating drafts, or offering grammar and style improvements.
- Personalized Experiences
  - ✓ Function: AI can tailor experiences to individual preferences, enhancing personalization and user engagement in creative and entertainment fields.
  - ✓ Examples:
    - o Streaming Services: AI algorithms recommend movies and shows based on user preferences and viewing history, enhancing the entertainment experience.
    - o Marketing Campaigns: AI-driven tools create personalized marketing content and advertisements based on consumer behavior and preferences.

7.2.3   IMPROVING EFFICIENCY AND PRODUCTIVITY

- Automating Repetitive Tasks
  - ✓ Function: AI can handle repetitive and mundane tasks, freeing up human workers to focus on more complex and strategic activities.
  - ✓ Examples:
    - o Administrative Tasks: AI systems automate scheduling, data entry, and document management, reducing the administrative burden on office workers.

- o Manufacturing: Robots and automation systems handle routine production tasks, increasing efficiency and allowing human workers to oversee quality control and complex operations.
- Enhancing Workflow
  - ✓ Function: AI can streamline workflows by integrating with existing systems and providing real-time assistance and recommendations.
  - ✓ Examples:
    - o Project Management: AI tools assist in managing project timelines, resource allocation, and task prioritization, helping teams stay organized and on track.
    - o Customer Service: AI-powered chatbots and virtual assistants handle common customer inquiries, enabling human agents to focus on more complex issues.

7.2.4 SUPPORTING COMPLEX PROBLEM-SOLVING

- Collaborative Problem-Solving
  - ✓ Function: AI can assist humans in solving complex problems by providing data-driven insights, simulations, and modeling.
  - ✓ Examples:
    - o Scientific Research: AI models simulate experiments and analyze research data, aiding scientists in discovering new insights and accelerating research processes.
    - o Engineering: AI assists engineers in designing and testing new products through simulations and optimization algorithms, enhancing innovation and reducing development time.
- Enhancing Cognitive Abilities
  - ✓ Function: AI tools can augment cognitive abilities by providing additional information, recommendations, and cognitive support.
  - ✓ Examples:
    - o Decision Support Systems: AI provides decision-makers with relevant data, forecasts, and scenarios to support strategic planning and problem-solving.
    - o Knowledge Management: AI systems help manage and retrieve knowledge from large datasets, making it easier for professionals to access relevant information and insights.

7.2.5 BRIDGING SKILL GAPS

- Skill Development
  - ✓ Function: AI can support skill development by providing training tools, resources, and personalized learning experiences.
  - ✓ Examples:
    - o Education: AI-driven educational platforms offer personalized learning paths, adaptive quizzes, and interactive content to help learners acquire new skills.
    - o Corporate Training: AI-powered training programs provide employees with tailored learning experiences and real-time feedback to enhance their skills.

- Accessibility
  - ✓ Function: AI can improve accessibility by providing tools and solutions for individuals with disabilities, enhancing their ability to interact with technology and perform daily tasks.
  - ✓ Examples:
    - o Assistive Technologies: AI-powered speech recognition and text-to-speech systems aid individuals with visual or hearing impairments in accessing information and communicating effectively.
    - o Adaptive Interfaces: AI-driven interfaces adjust to users' needs and preferences, providing a more accessible and personalized experience.

7.2.6   SUMMARY

AI and human collaboration can enhance decision-making, augment creativity, and improve efficiency across various fields. By automating repetitive tasks, providing valuable insights, and supporting complex problem-solving, AI complements human skills and enables greater productivity. Embracing AI as a collaborative tool rather than a replacement fosters innovation, bridges skill gaps, and enhances accessibility, leading to more effective and inclusive outcomes.

7.3   ETHICAL AI DEVELOPMENT

As AI technology advances, ensuring that it is developed and used ethically becomes increasingly important. Responsible AI development involves adhering to principles that promote fairness, transparency, and accountability while addressing potential risks and societal impacts. Here are key principles for guiding ethical AI development:

7.3.1   FAIRNESS AND NON-DISCRIMINATION

- Avoiding Bias
  - ✓ Function: AI systems should be designed to avoid and mitigate biases that could lead to discrimination against individuals or groups based on race, gender, age, or other characteristics.
  - ✓ Strategies:
    - o Diverse Data: Use diverse and representative datasets to train AI models to minimize the risk of bias.
    - o Bias Audits: Regularly conduct audits to identify and address biases in AI systems and their outputs.
  - ✓ Examples:
    - o Hiring Algorithms: Implementing checks to ensure that hiring algorithms do not discriminate against certain demographic groups.
    - o Credit Scoring: Ensuring that credit scoring models are fair and do not disproportionately impact marginalized communities.
- Equity in Access
  - ✓ Function: Ensure that AI technologies are accessible and beneficial to all individuals, regardless of socioeconomic status or other barriers.
  - ✓ Strategies:
    - o Inclusive Design: Develop AI solutions that are inclusive and consider the needs of underserved or vulnerable populations.

- o Affordable Access: Promote equitable access to AI technologies and their benefits.
- ✓ Examples:
  - o Healthcare AI: Making diagnostic tools accessible to under-resourced healthcare settings to improve health outcomes for underserved communities.
  - o Educational AI: Providing low-cost or free educational tools powered by AI to ensure broad access to learning resources.

7.3.2 TRANSPARENCY AND EXPLAINABILITY

- Clear Communication
  - ✓ Function: AI systems should be transparent about how they operate and make decisions, allowing users to understand the processes and outcomes.
  - ✓ Strategies:
    - o Explainable AI: Develop models and algorithms that provide clear explanations for their decisions and predictions.
    - o Documentation: Provide comprehensive documentation of AI systems, including their design, data sources, and decision-making processes.
  - ✓ Examples:
    - o Medical AI: Offering clear explanations of how AI diagnostic tools arrive at their conclusions, enabling doctors to understand and trust the results.
    - o Financial AI: Transparency in how credit scoring algorithms assess risk and make lending decisions.
- User Awareness
  - ✓ Function: Ensure that users are informed about the role of AI in systems and services they interact with.
  - ✓ Strategies:
    - o Disclosure: Clearly disclose when and how AI is being used in applications and services.
    - o Consent: Obtain informed consent from users when collecting and using their data for AI purposes.
  - ✓ Examples:
    - o Social Media: Informing users when AI algorithms are used to curate their news feeds or recommend content.
    - o Voice Assistants: Disclosing the use of AI in voice assistants and providing options for users to control data usage.

7.3.3 ACCOUNTABILITY AND RESPONSIBILITY

- Responsible Use
  - ✓ Function: Ensure that AI systems are used responsibly and that accountability mechanisms are in place for their outcomes.
  - ✓ Strategies:
    - o Clear Accountability: Define and assign responsibility for AI system design, deployment, and impact.
    - o Monitoring and Evaluation: Implement ongoing monitoring and evaluation to assess the impact of AI systems and address any issues that arise.

- ✓ Examples:
  - o Autonomous Vehicles: Establishing clear accountability for the safety and performance of self-driving cars, including protocols for addressing accidents or failures.
  - o Content Moderation: Ensuring accountability in AI systems used for content moderation on social media platforms.
- ▪ Ethical Governance
  - ✓ Function: Develop and adhere to ethical guidelines and governance structures that guide AI development and deployment.
  - ✓ Strategies:
    - o Ethics Committees: Form ethics committees or boards to review and oversee AI projects, ensuring adherence to ethical standards.
    - o Regulatory Compliance: Ensure compliance with relevant laws and regulations related to AI development and use.
  - ✓ Examples:
    - o AI Research Institutions: Establishing ethical review boards in research institutions to evaluate the potential impact of AI research.
    - o Corporate Policies: Implementing corporate policies that govern the ethical use of AI technologies within organizations.

7.3.4 PROVACY AND DATA PROTECTION

- ▪ Data Privacy
  - ✓ Function: Protect user privacy by implementing strong data protection measures and ensuring that AI systems handle data responsibly.
  - ✓ Strategies:
    - o Data Anonymization: Use data anonymization and encryption techniques to safeguard personal information.
    - o Consent and Control: Obtain explicit consent from individuals before collecting and using their data, and provide them with control over their information.
  - ✓ Examples:
    - o Healthcare AI: Ensuring that patient data used in AI systems is anonymized and protected to maintain privacy.
    - o Consumer Data: Providing consumers with clear options to manage their data preferences and privacy settings.
- ▪ Security Measures
  - ✓ Function: Implement robust security measures to protect AI systems and data from unauthorized access and cyber threats.
  - ✓ Strategies:
    - o Security Protocols: Develop and enforce security protocols to safeguard AI systems and the data they process.
    - o Regular Audits: Conduct regular security audits to identify and address vulnerabilities.
  - ✓ Examples:
    - o Financial Systems: Implementing advanced security measures to protect AI systems used in financial transactions and fraud detection.
    - o Smart Devices: Ensuring that AI-powered smart devices are secure from hacking and other cyber threats.

7.3.5   HUMAN-CENTRIC DESIGN

- Human Oversight
  - ✓ Function: Ensure that AI systems are designed with human oversight in mind, allowing humans to intervene when necessary.
  - ✓ Strategies:
    - o Human-in-the-Loop: Incorporate human oversight mechanisms in AI systems to enable human intervention and review of automated decisions.
    - o User Feedback: Allow users to provide feedback and appeal decisions made by AI systems.
  - ✓ Examples:
    - o Automated Hiring: Implementing human review processes in automated hiring systems to ensure fairness and address potential issues.
    - o Healthcare Diagnostics: Allowing medical professionals to review and validate AI-generated diagnostic recommendations.
- User Empowerment
  - ✓ Function: Design AI systems that empower users, giving them control over how AI interacts with them and their data.
  - ✓ Strategies:
    - o Customizable Features: Offer customizable features that allow users to tailor AI systems to their preferences and needs.
    - o Education and Training: Provide education and training to users on how to effectively use and interact with AI technologies.
  - ✓ Examples:
    - o Personal Assistants: Allowing users to customize settings and preferences in AI personal assistants to better meet their needs.
    - o Educational Platforms: Offering training on how to use AI-powered educational tools effectively.

7.3.6   SUMMARY

Ethical AI development involves adhering to principles of fairness, transparency, accountability, privacy, and human-centric design. By focusing on avoiding bias, ensuring clear communication, assigning responsibility, protecting data, and empowering users, organizations can develop AI systems that are responsible and beneficial for society. These principles guide the creation of AI technologies that are not only innovative but also aligned with ethical standards and societal values.

8 GETTING STARTED WITH AI

8.1 LEARNING RESOURCES

Venturing into the world of Artificial Intelligence (AI) can be both exciting and overwhelming. Fortunately, there are numerous resources available to help you get started. Here's a curated list of recommended books, online courses, and tools to build your foundational knowledge and skills in AI.

8.1.1 RECOMMENDED BOOKS

- For Beginners
  - ✓ "Artificial Intelligence: A Guide for Thinking Humans" by Melanie Mitchell
    - o Overview: A comprehensive and accessible introduction to AI, exploring its current state, capabilities, and future implications.
    - o Why Read: Provides a clear understanding of AI concepts and addresses common misconceptions.
  - ✓ "AI: A Very Short Introduction" by Margaret A. Boden
    - o Overview: An easy-to-understand overview of AI, including its history, development, and impact on society.
    - o Why Read: Ideal for those new to AI who want a concise yet thorough introduction.
- For Intermediate Learners
  - ✓ "Pattern Recognition and Machine Learning" by Christopher M. Bishop
    - o Overview: A detailed textbook on pattern recognition and machine learning techniques, including theoretical foundations and practical applications.
    - o Why Read: Offers a deeper dive into machine learning algorithms and their mathematical underpinnings.
  - ✓ "Deep Learning" by Ian Goodfellow, Yoshua Bengio, and Aaron Courville
    - o Overview: An authoritative book on deep learning, covering neural networks, training techniques, and practical applications.
    - o Why Read: Essential for those interested in the more advanced aspects of AI and deep learning.
- For Advanced Learners
  - ✓ "Artificial Intelligence: A Modern Approach" by Stuart Russell and Peter Norvig
    - o Overview: A comprehensive textbook covering a broad range of AI topics, from basic concepts to advanced techniques.
    - o Why Read: A cornerstone in AI education, offering an in-depth exploration of AI principles and methodologies.
  - ✓ "Reinforcement Learning: An Introduction" by Richard S. Sutton and Andrew G. Barto
    - o Overview: Focuses on reinforcement learning, a key area of AI, with detailed explanations of algorithms and practical applications.
    - o Why Read: Essential for understanding and applying reinforcement learning techniques in AI projects.

8.1.2 ONLINE COURSES

- Introductory Courses
  - ✓ "AI For Everyone" by Andrew Ng (Coursera)
    - o Overview: An introductory course designed for non-technical learners, covering the basics of AI, its applications, and societal impacts.
    - o Why Take: Great for those new to AI who want to understand its potential and implications without diving into technical details.
  - ✓ "Introduction to Artificial Intelligence" (Udacity)
    - o Overview: A beginner-friendly course that introduces fundamental AI concepts and practical applications.
    - o Why Take: Provides a solid foundation in AI, with practical examples and projects.
- Intermediate Courses
  - ✓ "Machine Learning" by Andrew Ng (Coursera)
    - o Overview: A highly popular course that covers machine learning algorithms, including supervised and unsupervised learning techniques.
    - o Why Take: Offers a comprehensive introduction to machine learning, taught by a leading expert in the field.
  - ✓ "Deep Learning Specialization" (Coursera)
    - o Overview: A series of courses focusing on deep learning techniques, including neural networks, convolutional networks, and sequence models.
    - o Why Take: Provides a detailed understanding of deep learning, with hands-on projects and practical applications.
- Advanced Courses
  - ✓ "Advanced Machine Learning Specialization" (Coursera)
    - o Overview: An advanced series of courses covering complex machine learning topics, including reinforcement learning and natural language processing.
    - o Why Take: Ideal for learners seeking to deepen their knowledge and expertise in advanced machine learning techniques.
  - ✓ "AI for Medicine" (Coursera)
    - o Overview: Focuses on applying AI to medical data, including diagnosis, treatment, and drug discovery.
    - o Why Take: Offers specialized knowledge in the intersection of AI and healthcare, with practical case studies and projects.

8.1.3 TOOLS AND PLATFORMS

- Development Frameworks
  - ✓ TensorFlow
    - o Overview: An open-source library developed by Google for building and training machine learning models, including deep learning networks.
    - o Why Use: Widely used for its flexibility and scalability in building AI models.
  - ✓ PyTorch
    - o Overview: An open-source machine learning library developed by Facebook, known for its dynamic computational graph and ease of use.

- o Why Use: Popular among researchers and practitioners for its intuitive interface and support for deep learning.
- ▪ Online Platforms
  - ✓ Kaggle
    - o Overview: A platform for data science and machine learning competitions, with datasets, notebooks, and tutorials.
    - o Why Use: Provides practical experience with real-world data and challenges, along with a supportive community.
  - ✓ Google Colab
    - o Overview: A cloud-based platform that allows users to write and execute Python code in a Jupyter notebook environment.
    - o Why Use: Offers free access to GPU and TPU resources, making it easier to experiment with machine learning models.
- ▪ Educational Resources
  - ✓ AI Hub (Google)
    - o Overview: A repository of AI resources, including models, datasets, and tutorials, provided by Google.
    - o Why Use: Offers a wealth of resources for learning and applying AI, with tools and guides from a leading AI research organization.
  - ✓ Microsoft Learn
    - o Overview: Provides interactive learning paths and modules on AI, machine learning, and data science.
    - o Why Use: Offers structured learning paths and hands-on labs for understanding and implementing AI concepts.

8.1.4   SUMMARY

Getting started with AI involves leveraging a combination of books, online courses, and practical tools. For beginners, books like "Artificial Intelligence: A Guide for Thinking Humans" and introductory courses on platforms like Coursera provide a solid foundation. Intermediate and advanced learners can benefit from more specialized texts and courses, such as "Deep Learning" and the "Advanced Machine Learning Specialization." Practical tools and platforms like TensorFlow, Kaggle, and Google Colab offer hands-on experience and resources to build and test AI models. By utilizing these resources, you can build a robust understanding of AI and its applications.

8.2   BASIC PROGRAMMING FOR AI

Programming is a crucial skill for working in Artificial Intelligence (AI), as it allows you to implement algorithms, build models, and process data. Among the various programming languages available, some are particularly well-suited for AI development due to their versatility, libraries, and community support. Here's an introduction to some of the most commonly used programming languages in AI, with a focus on Python, which is often considered the primary language for AI work.

8.2.1   PYTHON

- Why Python?
  - ✓ Ease of Use: Python is known for its clear and readable syntax, making it accessible for both beginners and experienced programmers.
  - ✓ Extensive Libraries: Python boasts a rich ecosystem of libraries and frameworks specifically designed for AI and machine learning, such as TensorFlow, Keras, PyTorch, and Scikit-learn.
  - ✓ Community Support: A large and active community provides a wealth of tutorials, documentation, and forums for problem-solving and collaboration.
- Key Libraries and Frameworks
  - ✓ NumPy: Provides support for large, multi-dimensional arrays and matrices, along with mathematical functions to operate on these arrays.
    - o Use Case: Essential for numerical computations and handling large datasets.
  - ✓ Pandas: Offers data structures and data analysis tools for handling and manipulating structured data.
    - o Use Case: Useful for data cleaning, transformation, and analysis.
  - ✓ Scikit-learn: A comprehensive library for machine learning that includes tools for data preprocessing, classification, regression, clustering, and model evaluation.
    - o Use Case: Ideal for building and evaluating machine learning models.
  - ✓ TensorFlow: An open-source framework developed by Google for building and deploying machine learning models, particularly deep learning models.
    - o Use Case: Supports a wide range of machine learning and deep learning tasks.
  - ✓ PyTorch: Developed by Facebook, PyTorch is a flexible and dynamic framework for deep learning that is favored for research and development.
    - o Use Case: Popular for developing neural networks and conducting research.
- Getting Started with Python
  - ✓ Basic Syntax: Learn Python's basic syntax, including variables, data types, control structures (if statements, loops), functions, and error handling.
  - ✓ Installation: Install Python and set up a development environment using tools like Anaconda, Jupyter Notebook, or PyCharm.
  - ✓ Practice: Start with simple programming exercises and gradually move on to more complex projects involving data manipulation and machine learning.

8.2.2   R

- Why R?
  - ✓ Statistical Analysis: R is particularly strong in statistical analysis and visualization, making it useful for data exploration and interpretation in AI projects.
  - ✓ Rich Packages: Includes packages like caret, xgboost, and randomForest for machine learning, and ggplot2 for data visualization.
  - ✓ Integration: R integrates well with other languages and tools, including Python, for hybrid approaches to data science.
- Key Packages

- ✓ caret: Provides a unified interface for training and evaluating machine learning models.
  - o Use Case: Simplifies the process of building predictive models.
- ✓ xgboost: An efficient and scalable implementation of gradient boosting for classification and regression tasks.
  - o Use Case: Commonly used in data science competitions for its high performance.
- ✓ ggplot2: A powerful visualization package that allows for complex and customizable plots.
  - o Use Case: Useful for creating insightful data visualizations.
- Getting Started with R
  - ✓ Basic Syntax: Familiarize yourself with R's syntax for variables, data structures (vectors, lists, data frames), and control flow.
  - ✓ Installation: Install R and RStudio, a popular integrated development environment (IDE) for R.
  - ✓ Practice: Work on data analysis projects and explore statistical models to build proficiency in R.

8.2.3 JAVA

- Why Java?
  - ✓ Performance: Java offers robust performance and is used in enterprise-level applications, including large-scale AI systems.
  - ✓ Libraries: Includes libraries like Weka and Deeplearning4j for machine learning and deep learning.
  - ✓ Scalability: Java's strong type system and performance make it suitable for building scalable AI applications.
- Key Libraries
  - ✓ Weka: Provides a collection of machine learning algorithms and tools for data mining tasks.
    - o Use Case: Useful for experimenting with machine learning algorithms and data preprocessing.
  - ✓ Deeplearning4j: An open-source deep learning library for Java and Scala, with support for neural networks and distributed computing.
    - o Use Case: Suitable for building deep learning models in Java environments.
- Getting Started with Java
  - ✓ Basic Syntax: Learn Java's syntax for object-oriented programming, including classes, objects, inheritance, and interfaces.
  - ✓ Installation: Set up Java Development Kit (JDK) and an IDE like IntelliJ IDEA or Eclipse.
  - ✓ Practice: Start with simple Java programs and gradually move on to implementing machine learning algorithms and models.

8.2.4 JULIA

- Why Julia?
  - ✓ Performance: Julia is known for its high performance and speed, especially in numerical and scientific computing.

- ✓ Ease of Use: Combines the ease of Python with the performance of C++, making it a strong choice for computational tasks.
- ✓ Libraries: Includes packages like Flux.jl for machine learning and DataFrames.jl for data manipulation.
- Key Packages
  - ✓ Flux.jl: A machine learning library that supports a variety of neural network architectures.
    - o Use Case: Provides tools for building and training machine learning models in Julia.
  - ✓ DataFrames.jl: Offers functionalities for data manipulation and analysis.
    - o Use Case: Facilitates data handling similar to Pandas in Python.
- Getting Started with Julia
  - ✓ Basic Syntax: Understand Julia's syntax for variables, functions, and data structures.
  - ✓ Installation: Install Julia and set up an IDE or notebook environment like Jupyter with Julia support.
  - ✓ Practice: Work on numerical computing tasks and machine learning projects to get accustomed to Julia's performance benefits.

8.2.5   SUMMARY

Getting started with AI programming involves choosing the right language and tools that align with your goals and interests. Python is widely recommended due to its readability, extensive libraries, and community support, making it ideal for most AI and machine learning projects. R is excellent for statistical analysis and data visualization, while Java is valuable for large-scale applications requiring high performance. Julia offers high performance for numerical computing tasks. Each language has its strengths and is suited to different aspects of AI development, so consider exploring multiple options to find the best fit for your projects and career aspirations.

8.3   EXPLORING AI PROJECTS

Diving into AI projects is a great way to gain hands-on experience and deepen your understanding of how AI works. Starting with simple projects allows you to explore fundamental concepts, experiment with different algorithms, and build a practical skill set. Here are some beginner-friendly AI projects and experiments to help you get started:

8.3.1   IMAGE CLASSIFICATION WITH MNIST

- Project Overview: Classify handwritten digits from the MNIST dataset using a neural network.
- Why It's Useful:
  - ✓ Concepts Covered: Image recognition, basic neural networks, classification.
  - ✓ Tools: Python, TensorFlow or PyTorch.
- Steps:
  - ✓ Download the MNIST Dataset: The MNIST dataset contains images of handwritten digits (0-9).

- ✓ Preprocess Data: Normalize images and split the dataset into training and test sets.
- ✓ Build a Neural Network: Create a simple feedforward neural network with one or more hidden layers.
- ✓ Train the Model: Use the training data to train the model and evaluate its performance on the test set.
- ✓ Evaluate Results: Assess the accuracy of the model and visualize some predictions.
- Resources:
  - ✓ TensorFlow MNIST Tutorial
  - ✓ PyTorch MNIST Example

8.3.2 SENTIMENT ANALYSIS OF MOVIE REVIEWS

- Project Overview: Analyze the sentiment (positive or negative) of movie reviews using natural language processing (NLP).
- Why It's Useful:
  - ✓ Concepts Covered: Text classification, NLP, sentiment analysis.
  - ✓ Tools: Python, Scikit-learn or NLTK.
- Steps:
  - ✓ Obtain Data: Use a dataset of movie reviews with labeled sentiments, such as the IMDB dataset.
  - ✓ Preprocess Text: Tokenize the text, remove stop words, and perform stemming or lemmatization.
  - ✓ Feature Extraction: Convert text into numerical features using methods like TF-IDF or word embeddings.
  - ✓ Train a Classifier: Use algorithms such as Logistic Regression, Naive Bayes, or Support Vector Machines to train a sentiment classifier.
  - ✓ Evaluate Performance: Measure accuracy and other metrics, and analyze some predictions.
- Resources:
  - ✓ NLTK Sentiment Analysis
  - ✓ Scikit-learn Text Classification Tutorial

8.3.3 PREDICTING HOUSE PRICES

- Project Overview: Predict house prices based on features such as size, number of bedrooms, and location.
- Why It's Useful:
  - ✓ Concepts Covered: Regression analysis, feature engineering, model evaluation.
  - ✓ Tools: Python, Scikit-learn.
- Steps:
  - ✓ Obtain Data: Use a dataset such as the Boston Housing dataset or Kaggle's House Prices dataset.
  - ✓ Preprocess Data: Handle missing values, encode categorical variables, and normalize numerical features.
  - ✓ Feature Engineering: Create new features or modify existing ones to improve model performance.

- ✓ Train a Regression Model: Use algorithms such as Linear Regression, Decision Trees, or Random Forests to predict house prices.
- ✓ Evaluate Model: Assess the model's performance using metrics like Mean Squared Error (MSE) or R-squared.
- Resources:
  - ✓ Scikit-learn Regression Tutorial
  - ✓ Kaggle House Prices Competition

8.3.4 BUILDING A SIMPLE CHATBOT

- Project Overview: Create a rule-based or machine learning-based chatbot that can handle simple conversations.
- Why It's Useful:
  - ✓ Concepts Covered: NLP, chatbots, intent recognition.
  - ✓ Tools: Python, NLTK, or Rasa.
- Steps:
  - ✓ Define Scope: Decide on the functionalities and topics the chatbot will handle.
  - ✓ Create a Knowledge Base: Develop a list of common questions and responses or use an existing dataset.
  - ✓ Implement Rules: For a rule-based chatbot, define patterns and responses. For a machine learning-based chatbot, use techniques like intent classification and entity recognition.
  - ✓ Build and Test: Implement the chatbot using a library like NLTK for basic text processing or Rasa for more advanced capabilities.
  - ✓ Refine: Test the chatbot and refine it based on user interactions and feedback.
- Resources:
  - ✓ NLTK Chatbot Tutorial
  - ✓ Rasa Chatbot Framework

8.3.5 RECOMMENDER SYSTEM

- Project Overview: Develop a recommender system that suggests items based on user preferences.
- Why It's Useful:
  - ✓ Concepts Covered: Collaborative filtering, content-based filtering, recommendation algorithms.
  - ✓ Tools: Python, Scikit-learn, or Surprise library.
- Steps:
  - ✓ Obtain Data: Use a dataset like MovieLens, which includes user ratings for movies.
  - ✓ Preprocess Data: Clean and prepare the dataset for analysis.
  - ✓ Implement Algorithms: Choose between collaborative filtering (based on user-item interactions) or content-based filtering (based on item features).
  - ✓ Evaluate Recommendations: Measure the effectiveness of recommendations using metrics such as Precision, Recall, or Mean Average Precision (MAP).
  - ✓ Deploy and Test: Implement the recommender system and test it with real users.
- Resources:
  - ✓ Scikit-learn Recommender Systems

✓ Surprise Library for Recommender Systems

8.3.6 SUMMARY

Exploring AI through simple projects provides practical experience and reinforces theoretical concepts. Starting with projects like image classification, sentiment analysis, house price prediction, chatbot creation, and recommender systems allows you to apply fundamental AI techniques and gain hands-on skills. Each project involves distinct concepts and tools, helping you build a diverse skill set in AI and prepare for more complex challenges.

9 CASE STUDIES AND REAL-WORLD EXAMPLES

9.1 SUCCESSFUL AI APPLICATIONS

AI has made significant strides in various industries, demonstrating its transformative potential through numerous success stories. These case studies highlight how AI technologies have been effectively applied to solve real-world problems, drive innovation, and create substantial value. Here are some notable examples:

9.1.1 NETFLIX'S RECOMMENDATION SYSTEM

- Overview: Netflix employs AI to personalize content recommendations for its millions of users, significantly enhancing user engagement and satisfaction.
- AI Technologies Used:
  - ✓ Collaborative Filtering: Analyzes user behavior and preferences to recommend content based on what similar users have liked.
  - ✓ Content-Based Filtering: Suggests content similar to what the user has watched in the past.
- Impact:
  - ✓ Enhanced User Experience: Personalized recommendations keep users engaged by suggesting relevant movies and TV shows.
  - ✓ Increased Engagement: Personalized suggestions contribute to higher watch time and subscription retention.
  - ✓ Business Growth: Netflix's recommendation system plays a crucial role in its success and user growth.
- Key Results:
  - ✓ Higher User Retention: The recommendation engine has significantly increased user retention rates.
  - ✓ Increased Viewing Time: Personalized content suggestions lead to longer viewing sessions.

9.1.2 IBM WATSON IN HEALTHCARE

- Overview: IBM Watson has been utilized to assist in diagnosing and treating diseases, providing doctors with valuable insights derived from vast amounts of medical data.
- AI Technologies Used:
  - ✓ Natural Language Processing (NLP): Extracts information from unstructured medical texts and research papers.
  - ✓ Machine Learning: Analyzes patient data to offer evidence-based treatment recommendations.
- Impact:
  - ✓ Improved Diagnostics: Helps in diagnosing rare diseases and identifying suitable treatment plans.
  - ✓ Personalized Medicine: Offers personalized treatment recommendations based on patient history and data.
  - ✓ Accelerated Research: Assists in identifying new drug candidates and understanding disease mechanisms.
- Key Results:

✓ Enhanced Accuracy: Improved diagnostic accuracy in oncology and other fields.
✓ Time Savings: Reduced the time required for research and diagnosis.

9.1.3 AMAZON'S ALEXA

- Overview: Amazon Alexa is a voice-activated virtual assistant that uses AI to understand and respond to user commands, perform tasks, and integrate with smart home devices.
- AI Technologies Used:
  ✓ Speech Recognition: Converts spoken language into text.
  ✓ Natural Language Understanding (NLU): Interprets user intents and processes commands.
  ✓ Machine Learning: Continuously improves the assistant's responses based on user interactions.
- Impact:
  ✓ Enhanced User Convenience: Allows users to control smart home devices, set reminders, and access information using voice commands.
  ✓ Integration with Services: Supports a wide range of third-party applications and services, extending its functionality.
  ✓ Market Leadership: Positioned Amazon as a leader in the voice assistant market.
- Key Results:
  ✓ High Adoption Rate: Alexa has become a popular choice for smart home assistants.
  ✓ Increased Device Sales: Boosted sales of Amazon Echo and other smart devices.

9.1.4 GOOGLE DEEPMIND'S ALPHAGO

- Overview: AlphaGo, developed by Google DeepMind, is an AI program that defeated the world champion Go player, demonstrating AI's capability in mastering complex games.
- AI Technologies Used:
  ✓ Reinforcement Learning: Trains the AI by playing numerous games against itself to improve its strategy.
  ✓ Neural Networks: Evaluates game positions and predicts optimal moves.
- Impact:
  ✓ Advanced AI Capabilities: Showcased the potential of AI in tackling highly complex and strategic tasks.
  ✓ Inspiration for Research: Spurred further research in AI and reinforcement learning techniques.
- Key Results:
  ✓ Historic Victory: Defeated the reigning world champion, Lee Sedol, in a series of games.
  ✓ Increased Interest: Generated significant interest and investment in AI research and development.

9.1.5 TESLA'S AUTOPILOT

- Overview: Tesla's Autopilot is an advanced driver-assistance system that uses AI to enable semi-autonomous driving capabilities, including lane-keeping and adaptive cruise control.
- AI Technologies Used:
  - ✓ Computer Vision: Analyzes camera feeds to detect objects, lanes, and road signs.
  - ✓ Machine Learning: Continuously improves driving algorithms based on data collected from Tesla vehicles.
- Impact:
  - ✓ Enhanced Driving Safety: Provides assistance in maintaining lane position and adapting speed based on traffic conditions.
  - ✓ Innovation in Automotive Industry: Positioned Tesla as a leader in autonomous driving technology.
- Key Results:
  - ✓ Increased Adoption: Widely adopted in Tesla vehicles, contributing to the company's growth.
  - ✓ Ongoing Development: Continuous updates and improvements through over-the-air software updates.

9.1.6 SUMMARY

These success stories illustrate the diverse applications and transformative impact of AI across various industries. From enhancing user experiences with personalized recommendations and virtual assistants to advancing medical diagnostics and autonomous driving, AI technologies are driving significant advancements and creating substantial value. By studying these cases, you can gain insights into how AI is being effectively utilized and explore potential applications in your own projects and endeavors.

9.2 LESSONS LEARNED

AI has made profound impacts across numerous industries, but with these advancements come valuable lessons. Understanding these insights can help organizations and individuals leverage AI more effectively and navigate challenges. Here's a look at key lessons learned from various AI implementations:

9.2.1 IMPORTANCE OF HIGH-QUALITY DATA

- Lesson: High-quality data is crucial for effective AI models. Inaccurate, incomplete, or biased data can lead to poor performance and unreliable results.
- Insights:
  - ✓ Data Collection: Ensure that the data collected is representative of the problem domain and diverse enough to capture different scenarios.
  - ✓ Data Cleaning: Implement thorough data preprocessing to remove inaccuracies, handle missing values, and normalize data.
  - ✓ Bias Mitigation: Regularly assess and address biases in the data to prevent skewed outcomes and ensure fairness.

- Example: In the healthcare industry, models trained on biased data may lead to less effective treatments for underrepresented populations. Efforts to use diverse datasets and implement fairness checks can improve outcomes.

9.2.2 CONTINUOUS LEARNING AND ADAPTATION

- Lesson: AI systems require ongoing updates and improvements to remain effective and adapt to new data and changing conditions.
- Insights:
  - ✓ Model Retraining: Regularly retrain models with new data to maintain accuracy and relevance.
  - ✓ Performance Monitoring: Continuously monitor model performance and address issues as they arise.
  - ✓ User Feedback: Incorporate user feedback to refine AI systems and enhance their usability and effectiveness.
- Example: Netflix's recommendation system benefits from continuous updates to its algorithms based on user interactions, ensuring that recommendations stay relevant and personalized.

9.2.3 TRANSPARENCY AND EXPLAINABILITY

- Lesson: AI systems should be transparent and their decisions explainable to build trust and facilitate understanding.
- Insights:
  - ✓ Explainable AI: Implement methods to make AI decision-making processes more interpretable, such as using explainable models or providing visualizations of decision factors.
  - ✓ User Communication: Clearly communicate the capabilities and limitations of AI systems to users and stakeholders.
  - ✓ Regulatory Compliance: Ensure that AI systems comply with regulations requiring transparency and accountability.
- Example: In financial services, explainable AI can help users understand why a loan application was approved or denied, leading to increased trust and satisfaction.

9.2.4 ETHICAL CONSIDERATIONS AND BIAS MANAGEMENT

- Lesson: Addressing ethical issues and managing biases is essential to ensure that AI systems operate fairly and responsibly.
- Insights:
  - ✓ Ethical Frameworks: Develop and adhere to ethical guidelines for AI development and deployment.
  - ✓ Bias Audits: Conduct regular audits to identify and mitigate biases in AI systems.
  - ✓ Inclusive Design: Engage diverse teams and stakeholders in the development process to ensure inclusivity and fairness.
- Example: AI-powered hiring tools have faced scrutiny for biased outcomes. Implementing diverse training data and bias detection mechanisms can help create more equitable hiring practices.

9.2.5 INTEGRATION WITH EXISTING SYSTEMS

- Lesson: Successful AI implementations require careful integration with existing systems and processes to ensure compatibility and effectiveness.
- Insights:
  - ✓ System Compatibility: Assess how AI solutions will interact with current infrastructure and workflows.
  - ✓ Change Management: Prepare for changes by training staff and adapting processes to incorporate AI effectively.
  - ✓ Scalability: Design AI systems with scalability in mind to accommodate future growth and evolving needs.
- Example: In retail, integrating AI-driven inventory management with existing supply chain systems can optimize operations and improve efficiency.

9.2.6 COLLABORATION AND CROSS-DISCIPLINARY TEAMS

- Lesson: AI projects benefit from collaboration among diverse teams, including data scientists, domain experts, and stakeholders.
- Insights:
  - ✓ Cross-Disciplinary Approach: Collaborate with experts from various fields to gain a comprehensive understanding of the problem and develop effective solutions.
  - ✓ Stakeholder Engagement: Involve stakeholders early in the process to align AI solutions with business goals and user needs.
  - ✓ Knowledge Sharing: Foster an environment of knowledge sharing and continuous learning to stay abreast of advancements and best practices.
- Example: Developing AI solutions for autonomous vehicles requires input from experts in machine learning, automotive engineering, safety regulations, and user experience.

9.2.7 REALISTIC EXPECTATIONS AND MANAGING COMPLEXITY

- Lesson: AI solutions should be designed with realistic expectations about their capabilities and limitations to avoid overpromising and underdelivering.
- Insights:
  - ✓ Scope Definition: Clearly define the scope of AI projects and set achievable goals based on current technology and resources.
  - ✓ Complexity Management: Address the complexity of AI systems through modular design and iterative development.
  - ✓ Risk Management: Identify potential risks and have strategies in place to mitigate them.
- Example: AI chatbots are often expected to handle a wide range of queries, but setting realistic expectations and focusing on specific use cases can lead to more successful implementations.

9.2.8 SUMMARY

The journey of implementing AI systems offers numerous insights and lessons. Key takeaways include the importance of high-quality data, continuous learning, transparency, and ethical considerations. Successful AI implementations require thoughtful integration, collaboration among cross-disciplinary teams, and realistic expectations. By applying these lessons, organizations can enhance their AI projects, drive innovation, and achieve meaningful outcomes.

10 CONCLUSION

10.1 SUMMARIZING KEY POINTS

As we wrap up our exploration of artificial intelligence (AI), it's essential to recap the major themes and takeaways that have shaped our understanding of this transformative technology. Here's a summary of the key points covered:

10.1.1 UNDERSTANDING AI

- Definition and Basic Concepts: AI involves creating machines and software that can perform tasks typically requiring human intelligence, such as learning, reasoning, and problem-solving. Core concepts include machine learning, deep learning, and neural networks.
- History and Evolution: AI has evolved from early rule-based systems to sophisticated neural networks and deep learning models. Milestones include the development of symbolic AI, expert systems, and recent advances in reinforcement learning and generative models.

10.1.2 WHY AI MATTERS

- Impact on Daily Life and Society: AI is transforming daily life by enhancing convenience, personalization, and efficiency. It affects various sectors, including healthcare, finance, transportation, and entertainment, contributing to improved quality of life and economic growth.
- Real-World Applications and Benefits: AI is applied in diverse areas such as smart assistants, recommendation systems, healthcare diagnostics, and autonomous vehicles. These applications demonstrate AI's potential to solve complex problems, enhance productivity, and drive innovation.

10.1.3 TYPES AND TECHNOLOGIES OF AI

- Narrow AI vs. General AI:
  - ✓ Narrow AI: Specialized in specific tasks, such as voice assistants and recommendation engines.
  - ✓ General AI: Hypothetical AI with generalized cognitive abilities comparable to human intelligence, still a subject of research.
- Key Technologies:
  - ✓ Algorithms and Models: Include neural networks, decision trees, and reinforcement learning algorithms.
  - ✓ Importance of Data: Data is fundamental for training AI models, affecting their performance and reliability.

10.1.4 APPLICATIONS IN EVERYDAY LIFE

- Smart Assistants and Chatbots: These tools use AI to understand and respond to user queries, automate tasks, and integrate with various services, making daily interactions more seamless.

- Recommendation Systems: Used by streaming services and online shopping platforms to suggest relevant content or products based on user preferences and behavior.
- Healthcare: AI enhances diagnostics and personalized medicine by analyzing medical data and offering insights for treatment and patient care.
- Autonomous Vehicles: AI powers self-driving technology, enabling vehicles to navigate and make decisions in real time using sensors, cameras, and machine learning.

10.1.5 THE POWER AND LIMITATIONS OF AI

- Strengths: AI excels in efficiency, scalability, and pattern recognition, enabling it to handle vast amounts of data and perform complex tasks with high accuracy.
- Limitations and Challenges: AI faces challenges such as biases in data, issues with data quality, and ethical concerns regarding decision-making and privacy. Addressing these limitations is crucial for responsible AI development.

10.1.6 ETHICAL AND SOCIETAL IMPLICATIONS

- Privacy and Security: AI raises concerns about data privacy and security, highlighting the need for robust protection measures and transparent practices.
- Bias and Fairness: Bias in AI systems can lead to unfair outcomes. It's essential to develop mechanisms to detect, mitigate, and prevent biases to ensure equitable and just results.
- Job Displacement and Economic Impact: AI may lead to job displacement in certain sectors but also creates new opportunities and drives economic growth. Addressing these changes requires proactive strategies for workforce adaptation and skill development.

10.1.7 THE FUTURE OF AI

- Emerging Trends: Advancements in AI research are paving the way for more sophisticated technologies, including improvements in general AI and increased integration with other emerging technologies like quantum computing.
- Human-AI Collaboration: AI is expected to complement human skills rather than replace them, enhancing productivity and creativity through collaborative approaches.
- Ethical AI Development: The future of AI involves developing responsible and ethical AI systems that prioritize transparency, fairness, and accountability.

10.1.8 GETTING STARTED WITH AI

- Learning Resources: There are numerous resources available for learning AI, including books, online courses, and tools that can help beginners build a strong foundation.
- Basic Programming for AI: Python is a widely used programming language in AI, known for its simplicity and powerful libraries for machine learning and data analysis.

- Exploring AI Projects: Engaging in practical projects such as image classification, sentiment analysis, and chatbot creation can provide hands-on experience and deepen understanding.

10.1.9 FINAL THOUGHTS

Artificial Intelligence is a rapidly evolving field with far-reaching implications across various domains. Understanding its core concepts, applications, strengths, and limitations is crucial for harnessing its potential responsibly and effectively. By staying informed about emerging trends and ethical considerations, we can navigate the future of AI with confidence and ensure that its benefits are realized in a fair and equitable manner.

10.2 FUTURE PROSPECTS AND ONGOING DEVELOPMENTS IN AI

As AI continues to advance, its future prospects and ongoing developments promise to bring transformative changes across various aspects of life and industry. Here's a glimpse into what lies ahead for AI, highlighting key areas of growth and innovation:

10.2.1 ADVANCEMENTS IN AI TECHNOLOGIES

- General AI and AGI (Artificial General Intelligence)
  - ✓ Objective: Developing AI systems with generalized cognitive abilities that can perform any intellectual task that a human can.
  - ✓ Current Status: While General AI remains a long-term goal, progress in areas like unsupervised learning and transfer learning is paving the way for more versatile AI systems.
  - ✓ Future Outlook: Research is focused on creating more flexible, adaptive, and intelligent systems that can understand and interact with the world more comprehensively.
- Advanced Machine Learning Models
  - ✓ Generative AI: Models such as Generative Adversarial Networks (GANs) are being refined to create more realistic images, videos, and text.
  - ✓ Self-Supervised Learning: Techniques that require less labeled data by leveraging unlabeled data to improve model training.
  - ✓ Neurosymbolic AI: Combining neural networks with symbolic reasoning to enhance the interpretability and reasoning capabilities of AI systems.

10.2.2 INTEGRATION WITH EMERGING TECHNOLOGIES

- AI and Quantum Computing
  - ✓ Objective: Leveraging quantum computing to solve complex problems faster than classical computers can, potentially accelerating AI training and optimization.
  - ✓ Current Status: Quantum computing is in its early stages, but research is progressing toward practical quantum processors.
  - ✓ Future Outlook: Integration of quantum computing with AI could revolutionize data processing, optimization, and problem-solving capabilities.
- AI and Edge Computing

- ✓ Objective: Bringing AI computation closer to the data source (edge devices) to reduce latency and improve real-time processing.
- ✓ Current Status: Edge AI is increasingly used in applications like autonomous vehicles, smart sensors, and IoT devices.
- ✓ Future Outlook: Enhanced edge AI will enable more efficient, real-time decision-making and reduce dependency on centralized cloud resources.

10.2.3 AI IN HEALTHCARE

- Personalized Medicine
  - ✓ Objective: Tailoring medical treatments and interventions based on individual patient data, including genetic, lifestyle, and environmental factors.
  - ✓ Current Status: AI is already being used to analyze genetic data and predict disease risks.
  - ✓ Future Outlook: Greater integration of AI with genomic research and electronic health records will drive more precise and personalized treatment options.
- AI in Drug Discovery
  - ✓ Objective: Accelerating the discovery of new drugs and therapies by predicting molecular interactions and identifying potential candidates.
  - ✓ Current Status: AI models are used to analyze biological data and simulate drug interactions.
  - ✓ Future Outlook: Improved algorithms and larger datasets will enhance the efficiency and accuracy of drug discovery processes.

10.2.4 ETHICAL AI AND RESPONSIBLE DEVELOPMENT

- Bias Mitigation and Fairness
  - ✓ Objective: Developing methods to detect, mitigate, and prevent biases in AI systems to ensure fairness and equity.
  - ✓ Current Status: Tools and frameworks are emerging to address bias and promote fairness in AI applications.
  - ✓ Future Outlook: Ongoing research and regulatory efforts will enhance the ability to create unbiased and equitable AI systems.
- AI Governance and Regulation
  - ✓ Objective: Establishing frameworks and guidelines for the responsible development and deployment of AI technologies.
  - ✓ Current Status: Various organizations and governments are working on AI ethics, governance frameworks, and regulatory policies.
  - ✓ Future Outlook: Comprehensive and globally harmonized regulations will be crucial for ensuring ethical AI practices and addressing societal concerns.

10.2.5 AI AND HUMAN COLLABORATION

- Augmented Intelligence
  - ✓ Objective: Enhancing human capabilities by using AI as a tool to support decision-making and creativity.
  - ✓ Current Status: AI is being used to assist in fields such as design, writing, and strategic planning.

- ✓ Future Outlook: Continued focus on human-AI collaboration will lead to more effective tools that complement and enhance human skills.
- AI in Education and Training
  - ✓ Objective: Leveraging AI to provide personalized learning experiences, automate administrative tasks, and enhance educational outcomes.
  - ✓ Current Status: AI-driven platforms are being used for tutoring, course recommendations, and learning analytics.
  - ✓ Future Outlook: AI will play a significant role in transforming education by offering tailored learning experiences and supporting diverse educational needs.

10.2.6 SOCIETAL IMPACT AND WORKFORCE TRANSFORMATION

- Job Creation and Transformation
  - ✓ Objective: Understanding how AI will create new job opportunities and transform existing roles across industries.
  - ✓ Current Status: AI is already impacting job roles in sectors like manufacturing, customer service, and data analysis.
  - ✓ Future Outlook: Continued evolution of AI will drive the need for new skills and roles, necessitating ongoing workforce adaptation and reskilling efforts.
- Economic Growth and Innovation
  - ✓ Objective: Leveraging AI to drive economic growth through increased productivity, new business models, and innovative solutions.
  - ✓ Current Status: AI is contributing to various sectors, boosting efficiency, and fostering innovation.
  - ✓ Future Outlook: AI will continue to be a major driver of economic development and technological advancement, shaping the future of global industries.

10.2.7 SUMMARY

The future of AI is filled with exciting prospects and ongoing developments that promise to shape various aspects of life and industry. From advancements in AI technologies and integration with emerging fields like quantum computing and edge computing to transformative impacts on healthcare, education, and the workforce, the trajectory of AI is both dynamic and promising. By focusing on ethical considerations, responsible development, and human-AI collaboration, we can harness the full potential of AI while addressing challenges and ensuring that its benefits are realized in a fair and inclusive manner.

11 APPENDICES

11.1 GLOSSARY OF TERMS

Artificial Intelligence (AI)

The simulation of human intelligence in machines designed to perform tasks that typically require human cognition, such as learning, reasoning, and problem-solving.

Narrow AI

Also known as Weak AI, it refers to AI systems designed to handle specific tasks or solve particular problems. Examples include voice assistants and recommendation systems.

General AI

Also known as Artificial General Intelligence (AGI), this is a theoretical form of AI that possesses generalized cognitive abilities comparable to human intelligence, capable of performing any intellectual task a human can do.

Machine Learning (ML)

A subset of AI that involves training algorithms to learn from and make predictions or decisions based on data. It enables systems to improve their performance over time without being explicitly programmed for each specific task.

Deep Learning

A specialized area within machine learning that uses neural networks with many layers (deep neural networks) to analyze complex patterns in large datasets. It is particularly effective in image and speech recognition tasks.

Neural Networks

Computational models inspired by the human brain, consisting of interconnected nodes (neurons) organized in layers. They are used to recognize patterns and make predictions based on input data.

Generative Adversarial Networks (GANs)

A type of deep learning model that consists of two neural networks—a generator and a discriminator—competing against each other to create realistic data, such as images or videos.

Reinforcement Learning

A type of machine learning where an agent learns to make decisions by performing actions and receiving feedback in the form of rewards or penalties. It is used in scenarios like game playing and autonomous driving.

Unsupervised Learning

A machine learning approach where models are trained on data without labeled responses. The system tries to identify patterns and relationships within the data, such as clustering or association.

Self-Supervised Learning

An approach where models learn from unlabeled data by creating their own supervisory signals. This method leverages the data itself to generate labels or targets for training.

Explainable AI (XAI)

Techniques and methods used to make the decisions and workings of AI systems more transparent and understandable to humans. This helps in building trust and facilitating interpretation of AI outputs.

Bias in AI

The presence of systematic errors or unfair treatment in AI systems due to biased training data or algorithms, which can lead to discriminatory outcomes or reinforce existing prejudices.

Ethical AI

The practice of developing and deploying AI systems in a manner that is responsible, fair, and aligned with ethical principles, including transparency, accountability, and respect for privacy.

Autonomous Vehicles

Vehicles equipped with AI systems that enable them to navigate and make driving decisions without human intervention, using sensors, cameras, and machine learning algorithms.

Recommendation Systems

AI algorithms used to suggest products, content, or services based on user preferences, behavior, and historical data.

Examples include those used by streaming platforms and online shopping sites.

Smart Assistants

AI-powered applications designed to help users perform tasks or obtain information through natural language interactions. Examples include voice assistants like Siri, Alexa, and Google Assistant.

Edge Computing

A computing paradigm where data processing is performed closer to the data source (edge devices) rather than relying on centralized cloud resources, often used to improve real-time performance and reduce latency.

Quantum Computing

An advanced type of computing that uses principles of quantum mechanics to perform complex calculations more efficiently than classical computers. It has the potential to significantly impact AI and data processing.

Personalized Medicine

An approach in healthcare where AI is used to tailor medical treatments and interventions based on individual patient data, including genetic, lifestyle, and environmental factors.

Bias Mitigation

Techniques and strategies employed to detect, reduce, and eliminate biases in AI systems to ensure fair and equitable outcomes for all users and applications.

Data Preprocessing

The process of cleaning, transforming, and preparing raw data for use in machine learning models. This includes handling missing values, normalizing data, and encoding categorical variables.

Model Retraining

The process of updating and refining a machine learning model with new data to maintain its accuracy and relevance over time as new information becomes available.

Human-AI Collaboration

The integration of AI systems with human capabilities to enhance decision-making, productivity, and creativity by leveraging the strengths of both humans and machines.

Neurosymbolic AI

An approach that combines neural network-based learning with symbolic reasoning to create AI systems that are both powerful and interpretable.

11.2 FURTHER READING

For those interested in delving deeper into the world of artificial intelligence (AI), here is a curated list of books, articles, and online resources that cover a range of topics from fundamental concepts to advanced applications:

BOOKS

"Artificial Intelligence: A Modern Approach" by Stuart Russell and Peter Norvig

"Deep Learning" by Ian Goodfellow, Yoshua Bengio, and Aaron Courville

"Superintelligence: Paths, Dangers, Strategies" by Nick Bostrom

"The Master Algorithm: How the Quest for the Ultimate Learning Machine Will Remake Our World" by Pedro Domingos

"AI: A Very Short Introduction" by Margaret A. Boden

"Human Compatible: Artificial Intelligence and the Problem of Control" by Stuart Russell

ARTICLES

"The Ethics of Artificial Intelligence" by Nick Bostrom and Eliezer Yudkowsky (2011)

"Deep Learning for Computer Vision: A Brief Review" by Rajalingappaa Shanmugamani (2020)

"The AI Winter: What It Is and How It Could Impact the Future of AI" by Michael Wooldridge (2019)

"The Impact of Artificial Intelligence on the Future of Work" by Daron Acemoglu and Pascual Restrepo (2018)

"The Road to Artificial General Intelligence: A Survey of State-of-the-Art Approaches" by François Chollet (2020)

ONLINE RESOURCES

Coursera: "Machine Learning" by Andrew Ng

edX: "AI for Everyone" by Andrew Ng

Kaggle: "Introduction to Machine Learning"

MIT OpenCourseWare: "Artificial Intelligence"

arXiv.org: "Artificial Intelligence"

Google AI Blog